AF876843

AN ESSAY ON ECONOMIC SYSTEMS

A TELEOLOGICAL APPROACH

By KAREL ENGLIS

Translated by

IVO MORAVCIK

EAST EUROPEAN MONOGRAPHS, BOULDER
DISTRIBUTED BY COLUMBIA UNIVERSITY PRESS, NEW YORK

1986

EAST EUROPEAN MONOGRAPHS, NO. CCI

PUBLISHED JOINTLY WITH THE CZECHOSLOVAK SOCIETY
OF ARTS AND SCIENCES (SVU)

The publication of this volume was made possible by the financial support of the Walter C. Koerner Fund of the Czechoslovak Society of Arts and Sciences.

Dr. Karel Englis:
Economic Systems

Published in April 1946 by the Association of Czechoslovak Lawyers "Vsehrd", Prague I, Parizska 27., within the framework of the Association of University Students. Printed by the printing house "Prace" in Prague with the print type cicero Excelsior.

Price 65 Kcs.

Copyright ©1986 by Czechoslovak Society of Arts and Sciences (SVU)
Library of Congress Card Catalog Number 85-82133
ISBN 0-88033-095-3

Printed in the United States of America

TABLE OF CONTENTS

PREFACE

This book fills an important void. For the first time it provides English-speaking social scientists, in particular economists, with an opportunity to acquaint themselves with the analytic methodology and theoretical conclusions of a prominent Czech economist.

But there is more here. In his Introduction Dr. Jaroslav Polach explains how some of Englis' key approaches, concepts and propositions relate to the mainstreams of evolving economic theory.

The translation of Professor Ivo Moravčík of the University of Alberta conveys ably and sensitively the author's often difficult conceptualizations.

Not infrequently, social scientists–including economists– are disappointed when their theories, even specific applicable aspects of those theories, fail to be adopted by policy makers in actual practice. In this respect Englis was more fortunate. His conceptions of socio-economic planning found application during the brief period 1945-48 in the policies of the Czech National Socialist Party, then led by Dr. Petr Zenkl. However, only a very discerning economic historian could ascertain the extent to which Englis' approaches met the test of reality in the all too brief period of post-war Czechoslovakia's developmental processes. Needless to say, the opportunity for testing Englis' theories came to an abrupt halt with the Communist Party's accession to monopoly power. Thenceforth an altogether different era of socio-economic policy had begun.

If recent economic theory–as Dr. Polach points out–has come to be grounded in systems analysis, teleological methodology and, indeed, a form of functionalist method, it is all for the better. For it would mean that Englis' work may be more relevant and more alive today than it might have been some decades ago.

This in no way suggests that today's economic theorists would somehow become Englis' "disciples". But it does indicate the saliency of the analytic modalities involved in his work, even if the propositions and conclusions driven by his methodological posture may well be culture- and time-bound and thus not necessarily applicable or acceptable in their original formulations.

This book has been long in the making. But time matters less when it comes to search for insight and understanding of fundamental issues that form an aspect, indeed a burden, of mankind's lasting heritage and are likely to remain of strategic importance in the future.

The Czechoslovak Society of Arts and Sciences is pleased to have the book published under its auspices, and on its behalf I wish to express appreciation to all who contributed to the project, in particular docent Ladislav Fuerst of Prague, Czechoslovakia who initiated the idea, Dr. Walter C. Koerner who assumed responsibility for carrying it out on this continent, to Dr. Jaroslav Polach, and to Professor Ivo Moravčík.

Pittsburgh, Pennsylvania
September 1986

Jiří Nehněvajsa, President
Czechoslovak Society of Arts and Sciences

INTRODUCTION

The translation of Karel Engliš' *Economic Systems,* by professor Ivo Moravčík offers a rare insight into "pure", rigorously theoretical analysis of the relationship between socio-political institutional frameworks and economic doctrines, and their implications for economic policy and specific economic developments. Although the origin of this inquiry may be traced to the experience of the late Karel Engliš, with economic structures as they evolved on the European continent, specifically in Czechoslovakia, the results of the study transcend the confines of any particular country.

The translation of *Economic Systems* had certainly been a difficult and exacting task. For one thing, it is not always easy to find appropriate counterparts for the author's concepts and terminology. They often depart iconoclastically from the accepted wisdom of conventional economics, either West, or East. Consequently, to grasp Karel Engliš' thoughts on economics requires that the reader should carefully follow his presentation with open mind and willingness to consider (though not necessarily to accept) his ideas. That requirement should be emphasized because it is known that economists do not favor radical departures from their own academic training, particularly if the new concepts are complex and require a considerable mental effort. After all, Keynes' *General Theory*[1] was considered by a large body of economists of his day as dull, poorly written and without significance.

Philosophically, Engliš' approach to economics is rooted in Immanuel Kant's system. This and his insistence on clearly defined concepts and consistent (deductive) logic in his search for a specific rationale in economics, was another factor why his theories were not sympathetically received by the "pragmatic", and notably the neoclassical, positivists among Anglo-American economists. Their disregard of broader social factors affecting economic policy and decisions (which conflicts strangely with their emphasis on economics as an empirical science) is one explanation for their position. Neglect of consistent methodology has been another obstacle to a more positive assessment of economic teachings—such as those of Karel Engliš—which emphasize that a clearly defined logical order of thought is a precondition for the understanding of economic phenomena and their analysis.[2]

The fact that Karel Engliš was a Czech and wrote mostly in Czech did not help in dissemination of his ideas either. Moreover, his written style, even in his native Czech, is rather complex and involved. His phraseology, often convoluted, was known to cause despair to his students, with the exception of those familiar with the regional peculiarities of his diction. Consequently, to make his *Systems* intelligible in translation took more than patient search for a corresponding terminology in English. The problem was not made easier for professor Moravčík by insistence of the author's literary executor that preference should be given to rigorously literary translation of Engliš' text.

Ivo Moravčík who undertook the translation is professor of economics at the University of Alberta in Edmonton, Canada. Fortunately, he had an opportunity to become acquainted with the fundamentals of Engliš' teachings when a young student at Charles University in Prague in pre-Communist days. Consequently, he has a better feel for what Engliš wanted to say and what often escapes those who only learn about his teachings from books. It also helped that Moravčík, after completing his training as economist in North America, concentrated on the study of comparative economics. That made him aware of the differences in economic development the world over and of the significance of the structure of economic activities in this process. Moravčík's writings, particularly his critical analyses of Marxian models and of reforms in socialist economies, made him naturally interested in Engliš' inquiry into the interdependence of economic doctrines and economic systems and their application to current issues of economic development.

The choice of Engliš' *Economic Systems* was clearly dictated by practical considerations. To translate Engliš' *opus magnum, System of*

Economics[3], would be a forbidding task, that would easily take years, perhaps a decade. Besides being not only much shorter, *Economic Systems* deals specifically with an aspect of economics that has been quite neglected in Anglo-American economics, Thorstein Veblen and Wesley C. Mitchell notwithstanding. Hence the translation of *Economic Systems* may also be viewed as an original contribution to the analysis of implications of institutional frameworks for basic economic concepts in Anglo-Saxon economics.

The fact that institutional economics has been neglected by Anglo-American economists is undoubtedly due to the relative stability of institutions in their part of the world. Defining economics as "a study of mankind in the ordinary business of life"[4], they could easily disregard the impact that institutions might have on economic behavior and thus also on economic analysis. With institutions changing only slightly and gradually, Anglo-American economists could, and did, consider the institutional framework as a long-term exogenous variable that is given and remains for practical purposes constant. In other words, institutional factors were considered–until recently–as insignificant for economic analysis which hardly ever extends over the life of one generation.

Even when a new approach to economic problems was made, as was the case with the Keynesian revolution, it was usually cast within the existing institutional framework. Thus British institutions of the thirties are the (implied) constant of *The General Theory*. In contrast, on the European continent political (and physical) revolutions called forth new economic theories. It was argued that theories could not be made effective without fundamental structural changes of institutional arrangements prevailing in a given body politic. It is therefore no wonder that on the Continent economics was predominantly "political economy" (national economy). Also, economic thought on the Continent was always closely related to the evolution of legal doctrines. It was recognized, however, that by replacing the principles of common law with codified bodies of laws, legislative enactment became the chief *raison d'être* of the nation-state, of its institutions, and thus also of the economic behavior of its population "in the ordinary business of life". As a result, economics on the Continent has been one of the disciplines of the "Staatswissenschaften". We should keep it well in mind, when reading or mulling over Engliš' *Economic Systems,* that the analysis is explicitly set within the order established in a nation-state.

Before turning to a more detailed discussion of the *Systems,* two other points should be brought to the reader's attention. First, I deal briefly with Karel Engliš' life and the most important factors that shaped his approach to economics. Second, and clearly intertwined with the former, is his thought-model: A Teleological Construction of Economics. This conceptual framework is a part of all Engliš' major writings. It is also—although only summarily treated—the basis of his *Economic Systems.* Hence it is essential for the understanding of *Economic Systems* that the reader should be acquainted with the main theses of Engliš' teleology. For this reason an outline, presented below (and originally published some time ago), is incorporated in this Introduction.

Karel Engliš was born in Hrabyň, near Opava in Czech Silesia on August 17, 1880.[5] His life-long interests in economics reflected issues that reverberated in social debates during his formative years. The 1880s and 1890s can be regarded as a most important period in the conceptual evolution of modern economics. It was during those years that—to mention only a few—Karl Menger published his treatise on marginal methodology that replaced the historical method as dominant tool of analysis in economics; that Boehm-Bawerk's *Positive Theory of Capital* appeared offering an alternative to Marx's theory of capital accumulation; that Walras' studies of market equilibrium ushered in the era of modern microeconomics; and that Marshall's *Principles* synthesizing the Continental developments with those of Jevons and other English economists became a point of departure for generations of economists in England, as well as the United States.

Engliš began his studies of economics (in conjunction with the law) under one of the first Czech economists, Professor Albín Bráf, at Charles University in Prague. He continued for two years in Munich, where he undoubtedly fell under the spell of the ideas of the prominent German institutionalist, Max Weber. It is obvious that Weber's search for a more logical process of analysis and epistemology in the social sciences was at the origin of Engliš' own continuous interest in these issues. It culminated in his development of teleology as the only appropriate and logically consistent methodology for economic analysis. It is a point of departure for inquiry into *Economic Systems.*

Engliš began his professional career at the Provincial Statistical Office for Bohemia in Prague, then continued in the Statistical Division of the

(Imperial) Ministry of Commerce in Vienna. During those years he was particularly interested in the statistical underpinnings of regulations in the area of social legislation. In effect, his experience with production and consumption statistics made his contribution essential for substantiating the regulations in terms of the goals of social, especially education policies. His work led to a number of monographs that he wrote on these questions. He was appointed professor of national economy at the Czech Technical University in Brno still during the days of Austria-Hungary.

After World War One, Engliš became professor of national economy and first Rector of the newly founded Masaryk University in Brno. It was chiefly during his teaching years that he developed his ideas about the modes of human cognition,[6] as related to economic phenomena. He was a prolific writer (for a Selected Bibliography of his writings, see Appendix), even though he served several times as the new Republic's Minister of Finance and from 1934 through 1938 as Governor of the Czechoslovak National Bank. He was widely credited with a number of successful policies that helped moderate the repercussions of the world economic crisis on Czechoslovakia.

During the Munich crisis, he was considered a potential candidate, acceptable to the major political parties, for the office of President. Engliš, however, chose to retire and devote his time to study and writing. During these years he wrote his books on *Logic,* and *Economic Systems.* Both were published after the war when he returned once again to Academia, this time as a professor of economics at Charles University in Prague. Once more the high office of University Rector was bestowed on him. When the Communists seized power in 1948, Engliš retired for the second time to Hrabyň but did not cease to pursue his academic interests. In 1957 he prepared a German version of his book on logic, while working on the preparation for publication of a German edition of his large study of the *System of Human Thinking.*[7] He died in the Summer of 1961.

Although his teachings were on the proscribed list during the Stalin era and for some years afterwards, interest in Engliš' economic analysis has been on the increase in Czechoslovakia ever since. Some, as for instance a member of the Governing Board of the Czechoslovak National Bank, Dr. František Vencovský of Prague, even suggest that Engliš' thought notably on planning, price theory, exchange rates, and monetary policy could be usefully applied in present day Czechoslovakia.[8] Also, Engliš' theories and their implications for various social sciences began to attract international attention chiefly due to Dr. Miloš Stádník and Ladislav A. Fuerst.[9] Yet, his last great work in the field of logic still awaits publication in Czechoslovakia (or for that matter anywhere else).

Faithful to his meticulous ways, Engliš began his inquiry into economic thinking[10] with an inquiry into logic.[11] To know how we generally formulate the systematic connection in our thoughts about and among the things of the world was, for Engliš, a step preliminary to any real understanding of the particular processes of individual scientific systems. From there on he proceeded to delineate the logical structure of economic thought so as to establish economics as a science in its own right. He saw the fundamental issue in this respect in the delineation of the subject of economics, that is, in defining the economic quality of our propositions and conclusions so that there would be a clear differentiation between economics and other social sciences. As he pointed out, none of the prevalent approaches could solve this problem because of the erroneous identification of the economic principle (that is, the particular rationality proper to economics) with economical characteristics, and, further, because only individual self-interest was considered to be this "economic-economical" rationality.[12]

Much like the German philosopher, H. Rickert, Engliš starts his inquiry with the proposition that it obviously cannot be the diversity of observed phenomena which makes for the diversity of sciences because the same phenomenon may be a subject of cognition and understanding of several logically ordered systems of thought, that is, of sciences.[13] In other words, one science does not appropriate the subject of its propositions and conclusions to the exclusion of another science; thus, for instance, an aspect of human conduct may be the subject of medical science as well as of law or economics. Ultimately, Engliš arrives at the conclusion that it is the mode of cognition and understanding which is the decisive criterion for constructing a separate body of scientific knowledge. This particular mode must be such as to assure a consistent logical procedure and also the sameness of the substantive content of the entire structure of propositions.[14] Consequently, he narrowed his task to finding the particular method by which we conceive and understand economic propositions.

Engliš' approach to this problem is essentially rooted in the Kantian dualism between the world which *is,* and the world which *ought to be;* i.e. the worlds of *Sein,* and *Sollen.*[15] That, however, does not mean Engliš believed there is another world in addition to that we assume we know exists. He accepted scientific *monismus* but what he did not accept is the assumption that to understand and explain phenomena in our world, we must conceive our propositions on only one level, namely that of existence. In other words, he rejected the idea that the only acceptable principle of scientific rationality is causality. Recognizing the validity of causal rationality in the area of existence Engliš argues that this method is not an appropriate mode of cognition and understanding for phenomena which involve human will, such as purposive acts of men. In such instances, a coherent and logically consistent conceptual framework may be constructed only if the principle of finality is employed. Accordingly, he then divides the entire scientific thought into two, respectively three, great categories.

One group includes all sciences whose logical structure of concepts is based on a descriptive explanation in terms of cause and effect. This is the world of ontological knowledge. In this cognitive process there is no true valuation since ontological qualities do not polarize and represent differences in degree only with respect to a conditionally accepted scale of measurement (e.g., temperature scale, etc.). The other group encompasses sciences which seek to understand and explain phenomena of the real world by conceiving them as "postulates", that is, as desirable for the realization of some purpose (*telos*).[16] This is the teleological rationality also called finality. Whereas in ontological cognition we look for cause and effect, teleological relationship is between purpose and instrument. Thus, one purpose may serve as an instrument, or a subordinated purpose to a higher, superordinated purpose. That means that the entire logical structure of thought in this group of sciences is teleologically ordered since human conduct is interpreted with respect to an anticipated postulated goal. Engliš, however, emphatically warns against assuming that the concept of a desired purpose is a psycho-physical act, which obviously can be the object of medical observation, though not of economics. The concept of purpose, as it is used in Engliš' theory, is a purely logical construction which simply imputes to a subject a certain desire. In other words, teleological method uses hypothesis which should explain a typical behavior, by hierarchically ordered postulates. To illustrate the difference between this and the principle of causality, under which we conceive of phenomena merely that they are or are not, Engliš suggests looking at the purposive phenomena through the lens of human interest.[17] What appears then is the spectrum of desires which reflect these interests and explain the transitive order of purposes as successive levels of instruments serving to advance the attainment of still another and higher goal, up to the primary purpose. Though it may be evident from what I have said up to now, I think I should underline that the teleological method as conceived by Engliš must not be identified with the search for an ultimate supernatural purpose and eternal truth.[18] For him, it is a method of cognition by which *human* behavior is understood and logically analyzed by means of a hierarchy of *human* purposes resulting from *human* volition. Engliš had no more use for the teleological approach as practised in the Middle Ages than had Bacon.

Of course, the imputation process is not limited to the purpose desired by an individual. It is obvious, though, that a postulated purpose which explains human purposive behavior can be equally well imputed to a social organization, particularly a state. This does not mean we should start analyzing the decision process of different societal groups in whose power it is to formulate and impose—by some established procedure—an overall social (national) purpose. Such analysis would be as much out of place here as the already rejected examination of an individual's psycho-physical act of desiring. On the other hand, once it is granted that a purposive human process may and should be also logically conceived and understood in a way that permits imputing a purpose to a societal decision, then significant theoretical ramifications emerge. It leads Engliš directly to his delineation of economic quality and fundamental dichotomy in economic models.[19]

Engliš derives economic quality, that is, the subject of economics, from the formal construction and material content of the primary *economic* postulate. He then defines such an *economic postulate* in two ways. On the one hand, when constructed by individuals, it is a personal ideal of satisfaction, and, on the other, when constructed by a societal process, it is some kind of objective ideal of the optimal development of society. Thus human purposive conduct motivated by either of the primary economic postulates thus formulated represents economic phenomena and is the subject of practical economic sciences. The logical and understanding process by which we arrive at our proposition hierarchically derived, i.e., teleologically organized, from the one or the other primary economic postulate constitutes economic theory.

Collaterally to the two fundamentally different primary economic postulates, we have, on one side, an economic theory in which economic phenomena are explained by individually postulated purposes. This is what we call an atomistic individualistic model. On the other side is a solidaristic system in which economic behavior is to be understood and explained only in relation to an over-all societal purpose. A *caveat* is advisable here, however, in order to avoid identifying this social purpose as a simple summation of individual purposes because these, being subjective, are neither comparable nor additive. The societal purpose, on the contrary, is objective, does not depend on a subjective evaluation, and is objectively communicable and comparable. It is obvious that between those two theoretical extremes, mixed systems, as, for instance, the national cooperative system are also possible.

Let me now turn briefly to concepts of utility, scarcity, and economic goods to see how they are affected by this methodological division. Generally speaking, as Engliš points out, utility or scarcity and the related concept of economic goods do not exist on the level of ontological knowledge. Utility or disutility, scarcity or abundance are economic qualities of acts and things (goods) which cannot be conceived without teleological thinking because they derive their conceptual validity only from a purpose for which they are demanded as instruments (intermediary purposes).[20] Evidently then, a notion of utility, etc., as seen in an individualistic model sharply differs from its synonym derived from the solidaristic economic primary purpose. Moreover, the transitive character of purposes *within each model* accounts for the similarly changing pattern of utilities, cost, scarcities, etc., although within one model they are all linked together by the hierarchy of superordinated purposes, and ultimately the primary postulate, so as to form an organic totality of purposes (*věcná solidarita účelů*).[21] The cost is, in effect, an amount of disutility incurred when procuring (producing) an instrument necessary to the realization of a desired purpose. The cost is a logical construction, not psycho-physical disutility, and must always be construed with respect to the same purpose as is utility evaluation, though in the opposite direction. This by itself excludes the validity of the notion of foregone opportunity as an alternative cost because (1) the foregone opportunity does not affect utility evaluation derived from a given purpose, i.e., it does not create any disutility; (2) it is a logically inconsistent intermingling of utility and cost considerations. The latter analyzes alternative disutilities created in the different ways by which an instrument for a *given postulate* can be produced (procured); the former considers alternative utilities resulting from the application of a *given instrument* to different postulates.

From the organic solidarity of purposes, which is contingent on maximization of the primary purpose, results a process of equilibrating relative marginal utilities of different intermediary purposes (instruments). The equilibrating factor, once more, is the purely logical concept based on the teleological structure of economic propositions rather than a derivation from a psychic act as envisaged in the Austrian School, which is based on the operation of Gossen's laws. Moreover, as Engliš points out, he is speaking about the *relative* marginal utilities of different purposes (instruments) and not about the absolute "Grenznutzenniveau" of the Austrian School.[22]

Needless to say, there are still other significant facets of Engliš' ideas, but the limited scope of this Introduction precludes their examination. Still I hope that I have sufficiently elucidated what Engliš considered the paramount result of his analysis, that is, the apodictic relationship between economic theory and teleological method.

The Scope and Nature of Economic Systems

Let us first note that the notion of a system always involves a purposive organization.[23] Seen from that point of view, an economic system is a purposive organization *par excellence,* since economic decision-makers determine the alternative ways and their time sequences for allocating available scarce resources to competing purposes. Moreover, as Engliš emphasizes, the concept of economic system is necessarily tied to another, societally-dominating purposive organization, the nation-state. This relationship and its implications for a conceptual delineation of economic rationality (discussed below) is the key to the understanding of *Economic Systems.*

In this context, Engliš emphasizes that he is concerned only with the modern nation-state whose primary purpose, as he postulates it, is to exercise care for the economic welfare of its population. It is the nation-state's political and legal formulation of the scope and nature of this primary purpose (i.e., what is economic welfare of its people) that establishes a structure of interrelated economic purposes. The characteristics of this structure reflect a particular economic system. Furthermore, the structural hierarchy of interrelated sub- and super-ordinated economic purposes, derived from the primary purpose, delineates a normative framework for economic decisions and activities within the given nation-state.

Economic rationality, i.e., the logical conceptualization of the most rational ways to allocate in time and to competing purposes available resources so as to fit the established hierarchy of purposes, clearly depends on the structure of the system. For example: A particular allocation of resources may be found, according to one concept of economic rationality pertaining to one economic system to be "useful", i.e., to increase the economic welfare of the population. Yet, the same allocation under a differently structured purpose of economic activities, and economic rationality derived from it, may be deemed as not "useful", detracting, in fact from the economic welfare of people.

The proposition that the concept of economic rationality is system-determined and must be derived from the particular final purpose of economic decisions and activities is an essential premise of Engliš' theory of economic systems. Accordingly, the notion that economic rationality is an unchangeable category corresponding to some natural-law principles established on the basis of an ontological analysis of economic phenomena is rejected. Instead, as already indicated above, one must employ teleological methodology, analyzing and explaining economic decisions and activities in terms of teleological rationality relating such decisions and activities to the purposes to be attained.

On a purely theoretical level, Engliš recognizes two categorically polarized economic systems. In one, the nation-state leaves it to individuals to formulate their own, subjective, hierarchy of sub- and super-ordinated purposes, as well as the activities and their distribution over time which maximize utility, satisfaction, profit, etc.) derived from the allocation of resources to competing purposes under the conditions of market competition.

In this free-market system, overall economic welfare of the population is an aggregate of individual, subjectively determined, utilities. The role of the nation-state in individual economic decisions and activities is, as Engliš sees it, rather passive. It is up to each individual to take care of his own economic well-being. The state only sees to it that there are no impediments preventing individuals from pursuing their own economic goals.

This is, of course, what we know as an individualistic economic system based largely on a "laisser faire" philosophy. In Engliš' presentation this system has two sub-systems: The capitalist system, and the system of economic cooperation. The former is characterized by profit-seeking capitalist enterprise and the market mechanism; the latter by cooperation of consumers, producers, sellers, etc. in an economic entity replacing the profit-seeking enterprise with cooperative organization whose members share in economic benefits on the basis of their proportionate labor contributions. There exist other substantive differences in the attributes of both systems. However, the individualistic determination of the structure of purposes in the two sub-systems is for Engliš decisive for their classification as individualistic economic systems.

On the opposite pole lies what Engliš identifies as the solidaristic (or communist) system. Here the final purpose and the corresponding hierarchy of subordinated purposes, as well as their time distribution are determined by a societal formulation of the scope and nature of the national economic welfare. Or, as Engliš points out, in this system the nation-state substitutes its own, objectively established concept of economic welfare for that of individuals. In Engliš' parlance, in the solidaristic economic system, individuals are the objects of care of the nation-state in accordance with some objectively established criteria of their economic needs. In individualistic systems they take care of their own economic well-being, according to their subjectively perceived wants.

Of course, in practice these theoretically pure, polarized economic systems occur in a number of mixed variations. But as Engliš insists, correct identification of respective elements in the mixed systems is a condition of proper understanding of their implications for economic decisions, valuation of their results, and appropriate choice of policy options. This is well demonstrated in Engliš discussions of variations of economic goods, or the role of money in different economic systems.

The differences of valuation in the two years can be shown by the following example. In an individualistic economic system, the sum (usually expressed in per capita terms) of individual, partial, well-beings established on the basis of equi-marginal rationality, is the measure of the overall welfare of the population. As a consequence if the population increased its use of tobacco to, say, three packs of cigarettes per day, GNP would rise, *ceteris paribus,* not only by the increment in expenditure on cigarettes but also by additional investment of tobacco farmers, plus the increased spending by ancillary industries and the greater number of employees. Indeed, GNP would also increase because of increased expenditures on medical and funeral services. This is a contradiction outcome of economic analysis purporting that economic welfare (measured by GNP) increases as more people become ill and die due to increases in certain kinds of expenditure. This is a logical conclusion of economic positivism which holds that economics is a value-neutral science.[24]

On the other hand in a solidaristic system, provided that its primary purpose is formulated to include maintenance of good health of people, expenses for cigarettes would be seen as opposed to this societally established goal. Consequently resources and labor would be transferred from tobacco growing and cigarette making industries to other economic activities deemed more "valuable" from the viewpoint of the primary purpose. *Ceteris paribus,* the social product in such solidaristic system might be smaller than GNP as measured by traditional methods.

The concepts of economic rationality and the related notion of economic efficiency, that would correspond to the polarized dichotomy of economic systems are stated by Engliš in terms that require an explanation. On the one hand, he speaks of a *nexus,* i.e., a particular relational bond between economic goods and services in individuals' decisions to allocate them so as to maximize their economic goals. I refer to this linkage as the *inter-commodity nexus.*

On the other hand, there is a *nexus* that characterizes solidaristic rationality. This is a relational bond between persons and the final purpose, i.e., societally defined economic welfare in a nation-state. For lack of a better term, I call it an *interpersonal nexus.*

The analytical significance of these concepts can be grasped and appreciated much more easily once we realize that the nexus, as Engliš uses the term, is a specific *functional* relationship. It relates in a specific way the use of scarce resources, including human resources, to maximize economic welfare within the hierarchy of economic purposes of a given economic system. This specific, though differing functional relationship reflects economic rationality, as well as efficiency, typical for the economic system in question.

In effect, we may view the inter-commodity nexus, i.e., the economic rationale for the allocation of resources in the individualistic system, as the equi-marginal principle (whether referring to the marginal ratio of prices to utility, or costs to revenues, etc.). Individuals make economic decisions according to the equi-marginal principle in an effort to maximize their economic goals, whether these are in terms of utility or profit. We may substitute the marginal rate of substitution as the equi-marginal principle corresponding to the inter-commodity nexus.

The inter-personal nexus of the solidaristic system is more difficult to explain in terms of conventional economics. However, relying on a paradigm introduced by Von Bertalanffy in his *General System Theory*[25], we may equate Engliš' inter-personal nexus with Bertalanffy's concept of *equi-finality.* For our purpose we may express it as a functional relationship which the nation-state establishes between its intial human and other resources, on the one hand, and the societally determined final purpose, on the other hand. The equi-finality principle seeks to find alternative options which equalize, at the margin, relative contributions of the nation's resources to maximize societally determined economic welfare in the nation-state.[26]

It may be practical to stress again, what should be quite obvious by now, that under the equi-finality principle, the valuation of human and other resources is quite different from that arrived at under the equi-marginal principle. Correspondingly, economic efficiency (in the deployment of resources) is quite different in one system than the other.

I have dealt with these concepts of Engliš at some length, because once we understand his differentiation of economic rationality (and economic efficiency) as derived from the hierarchy of either individualistic or solidaristic purposes, it is easy to follow his further discussion of economic systems and their attributes. A synoptic table in Chapter V of the book is most helpful in this regard as it offers a comparitive review of the most important elements and the varying policy implications in each system.

One other point still worth mentioning concerns the relationship of ethical and economic systems discussed by Engliš in Chapter VII. Given the nature of humans and the prevailing ethical codes, he finds that people prefer individualism when it comes to production of material wealth, but when in need they seek rescue in solidaristic arrangements. However, he concludes that longing for freedom is the greatest adversary of the solidaristic (communist) system.

Concluding Comments

No doubt, a number of questions could be raised regarding one or the other aspect of Engliš' teleological conceptualization of economic systems. For one thing, his apodictic style, insistence on the exclusivity of his ideas and their absolute validity was due to evoke, as in fact it did, acute aversion to his thoughts. Others found it difficult to accept his theory because of the confounding complexity of the concepts of teleological methodology and doubts as to its appropriateness for scientific inquiries.

It might have been useful for understanding his *Economic Systems*, (at least by Anglo-American economists), had Engliš employed a few mathematical formulae rather than lengthy discussions of the functional relations characterizing economic systems. A mathematical model of a general system used by L. von Bertalanffy is an example of a possible alternative approach.[27]

Also, the fact that Engliš finalized his thoughts on economic systems in intellectual isolation during World War II prevented him to test his theories in discussion with his peers. This probably accounts for some baffling discrepancies such as in Chapter II, p. 9. In discussing the solidaristic system, Engliš observes that in addition to the inter-personal nexus, (nexus of personal solidarity), according to which allocation of resources is optimized in that system, recourse is also made to the inter-commodity nexus (nexus of material solidarity). But since the former is based on an objectively and the latter a subjectively established hierarchy of economic purposes, their simultaneous application in a theoretically pure solidaristic model is logically in conflict with Engliš' own delineation of the economic rationality particular to each of these systems.

Some, as professor William Jaffe[28], regard Engliš' *Economic Systems* as reflecting only his own subjective and moral attitiudes. As a consequence, they consider Engliš' theory as not generally valid and ill-fitted for inquiries into economic systems. Still others see Engliš' *Systems* as hardly anything else than an axiomatic work of little analytical value.

By now, however, most of these objections have lost their relevance. The evolution of economics since the 1950s has brought the mainstream of economic analysis closer to Engliš' teleological thought-model and his conceptualization of economics. The reasons for this development are manifold.

Among them is a strong interest in general system theory and its application to scientific inquiries. The theory fully endorses Engliš' main premise that a teleological method is one of possible approaches to scientific inquiries. Moreover, system theory also supports his position that teleological methodology is the only appropriate one for analyzing purposive organizations such as economic systems.[29]

Take another of Engliš' propositions, that the framework of economic systems, and thus of economic analysis, is pre-determined by the structure of purposes derived from the primary purpose which the nation-state established for economic decisions and activities.[30]

Because of the infatuation of neo-classical, positive economics with an analogy between economic phenomena and 19th-century physics, its ontological cognitive process and mechanical causality laws, economists of this school were unwilling to consider a teleological relationship between economics and the nation-state.

That, of course, has been changing. In 1973 Paul Samuelson referred for the first time in the ninth edition of his renown, long-running series on positive economics to "political economy," rather than simply to "economics."[31] Other authors too now acknowledge that the principles of economic analysis, for instance of such central part of positive economics as price theory, are valid only within the purpose structure of a given nation-state.[32]

However, it is in the field of welfare economics that the significance of the nation-state goals for economic rationality and efficiency has been most fully recognized. This is reflected, for instance, in the writings of William Baumol.[33] However, compared to Engliš' thought on this subject, welfare economics still suffers from some confusion because of the failure to differentiate between the normative nature of law and the teleological construction of economics.[34]

It is no wonder that an inherent inability of "standard" economics (as Nicolas Georgescu-Roegen refers to the school of neo-classical positive economics)[35] to provide meaningful answers to actual economic problems has been most clearly established in the economics of natural resources.

Unless carried on within the legal framework of a given territorial body politic and in interface with an established hierarchy of economic purposes, economic analysis of natural resources is meaningless. In true analogy to mechanistic causality and ontological methodology such analyses are also static. In contrast, teleological methodology is future-oriented by the logic of the meaning of purposes. Therefore, teleological analysis has an inherent predictive quality and is therefore well suited for formulation of meaningful economic options in the field of natural resources. Nowhere is that aspect of the teleological approach better demonstrated, even if not identified as such, than in the book of John V. Krutilla and Otto Eckstein, *Multipurpose River Development: Studies in Applied Economic Analysis*.[36]

It is characteristic of teleological analysis that—as Engliš explains—economic decisions and activities leading away from a given hierarchy of purposes should be seen as decreasing the primary purpose, i.e., economic welfare (whether defined societally or as an aggregate of individual economic well-beings). In other words, GNP as currently defined cannot be considered a meaningful index of economic welfare. This is also the idea behind the model of NEW, i.e., Net Economic Welfare index, arrived at by deducting "disamenities" (disutilities or losses in the quality of life, etc.) from GNP, as proposed by William Nordhaus and James Tobin.

Yet, and despite the fact that various teleological concepts formulated by Engliš half a century ago are being incorporated in one way or another into current economic thought and analysis, they are still treated as a kind of aberration. This is shown, e.g., in "A Reconsideration of the Theory of Value" by Sir John Hicks.[37]

To a degree it is surprising that the Justices of the U.S. Supreme Court rather than economists had a better grasp of the idea that economic efficiency must be evaluated in relation to the hierarchy of purposes within which economic decision and activities are carried on, i.e., that it is incorrect to regard economic efficiency within one economic system as an absolute yardstick, so that economic efficiency corresponding to economic criteria and structure of purposes is seen as a kind of aberration.

This is illustrated in a number of decisions, notably in *Brown Shoe Co. v. USA*.[38] Here the Court rejected the idea that individual economic efficiency is a controlling criterion for economic decisions and activities subject to the Sherman Antitrust Act. The primary purpose of the Act is to secure economically viable survival of small, independent tradesmen and craftsmen as the backbone of the Republic. Consequently the Court found the restrictions imposed on economic decisions and activities by the Sherman Act cannot be defeated in the name of individual economic efficiency. Restated in somewhat more traditional terms, one may say that economic efficiency established under an objective function of, say, common defense excludes the relevance of objections made on the grounds of individual economic efficiency and individual material welfare.

It is ironic that in the course of this evolution of economic ideas during the last 50 years the thought of Karel Engliš has never been mentioned outside the European continent particularly outside Central Europe.[39] He has remained almost completely unkown to English-speaking economists except for a rather short obscure reference.[40]

The purpose of this book is to correct, at least partially, this situation. Professor Moravčík's translation of *Economic Systems* provides English-speaking economists with an opportunity to peruse Engliš' ideas on economic structures as he himself presented them. Their overview in this Introduction is set against the background of continuous evolution in economic analysis. I hope it will help in understanding not only the innovative quality of Engliš' thought and methodological consistency of his *Economic Systems* but also in their powerful predictive capacity, especially in the area of economic policy.

Though professor Moravčík bears sole responsibility for the translation of *Economic Systems,* it is nevertheless a joint product of many individuals and institutions. Only a few are mentioned here, though the number of those who had contributed their time and effort is much larger.

The idea to translate *Economic Systems* into English originated with docent Ladislav A. Fuerst, Karel Engliš' literary executor and faithful propagator of his work beyond Central Europe. While work on the translation went on, docent Fuerst consulted with professor Moravčík both by correspondence and during the latter's visits in Czechoslovakia.

On the North American continent the project found an active supporter in Dr. Walter C. Koerner, industrialist, philantropist and member of the Czechoslovak Society of Arts and Sciences (SVU) of Vancouver, British Columbia, Canada. Dr. Koerner was a personal friend of Karel Engliš during his early career in the forest products industry while residing in Opava, close to Engliš' birthplace of Hrabyň. They shared many interests, in particular the development of Czechoslovakia's trade industry and Dr. Koerner admired Engliš as a great humanist and educator, one of the personalities who made Czechoslovakia a beacon of democracy in Central Europe between the two World Wars.

The Czechoslovak Society of Arts and Sciences (Společnost pro Vědy a Umění, SVU), an international society of scholars and artists, assumed sponsorship of the publication. Its president, professor Jiří Nehněvajsa of the University of Pittsburgh was instrumental in interesting Columbia University Press and the editor of its East European Monographs, professor Stephen Fischer-Galati of the University of Colorado in publishing the book.

July 1986

Jaroslav G. Polach
Ph.D., Dr. Jur.
Senior Research Associate
University of Pittsburgh

NOTES

1. *The General Theory of Employment*, Interest and Money. London: MacMillan and Co., Ltd.; first published in 1936.

2. See particularly Joseph A. Schumpeter, *History of Economic Analysis*. New York: Oxford University Press, 1955, pp. 7-30; also Emile James, *Histoire de la pensée économique au XXe siècle*. 2 vols. Bibliotèque de la science économique. Paris: Presses Universitaires de France, 1955. Vol. 2 Ch. V.

3. A massive, two-volume *Soustava národního hospodářství* was published in Prague by Melantrich in 1938, just before the political upheavals, leading to the Second World War, engulfed Czechoslovakia. This undoubtedly was also the reason why this life-achievement of Karel Engliš has remained largely unknown. For other of his writings see the Appendix to this Introduction.

4. Alfred Marshall, *Principles of Economics*. Eighth Edition. New York: The MacMillan Company, 1952; Bk. 1, Section 1; Marshall's definition was selected here because of the importance of the Marshallian approach in Anglo-American economics before the "winds of change" set in.

5. The following is based chiefly on material provided by Docent Ladislav A. Fuerst of Prague, executor of Karel Engliš' literary legacy, to Dr. Walter C. Koerner of Vancouver, Canada, Engliš' long-time friend, who made this SVU publication possible.

6. See, for instance, Ladislav Fuerst, "Karel Engliš, Kantův apriorismus a myšlenkový řád" ["Karel Engliš, the Apriorism of Kant and the Order of Thought"] *Filosofický Časopis*, Czechoslovak Academy of Sciences, 1967, No. 4, pp. 531-543. The paper includes interesting notes on some of Engliš' works still not published - e.g., his *Velká Logika* [*Major Logic*], (contrasted with his *Lesser Logic*, published by Melantrich, Prague, 1947).

7. The German version of *Lesser Logic* was published under the title *Das Problem der Logik*. Wien: Rudolph M. Rohrer Verlag, 1960

8. František Vencovský, "Karel Engliš" in the series *Profily Známých Edonomů* [Profiles of Well Known Economists]; pp. 380-384 [Prague, 1970?].

9. The late Czech economist, Miloš Stádník, then of Prague and later of Harvard University delivered papers on Engliš' contribution to national income theory at an international conference in Eire in 1967. L. A. Fuerst of Prague, probably the greatest expert on Karel Engliš, presented a paper on "Die juristische Argumentation im Lichte der Legischen Erkentnisstheorien," at the World Congress for Law and Social Philosophy, Brussels, 1971. This paper was a follow-up of a study of Engliš' cognition theories presented at the earlier conference in 1967. After having critically examined the normative theory of law (of Hans Kelsen and Frantisek Weyr) in its interface with Engliš' teleology, Fuerst suggests that we consider a further extension of the logical categories of human cognition, in addition to those that Karel Engliš suggested.

10. A more detailed account can be found in Jaroslav G. Polach, "Teleological Construction of Economics: Professor Karel Engliš' Contribution to Economic Thought" in *The Czechoslovak Contribution to World Culture*. Miloslav Richcígl, Jr., Ed., The Hague: Mouton & Co., 1964; pp. 329-340. That study is chiefly based on the following works of Engliš: *Teleologie jako forma vědeckého poznání* (Praha, F. Topič, 1930); *Soustava národního hospodářství* (Praha, Melantrich, 1937), Vol. 1, pp. 6-163; *Teorie hodnoty a hodnocení* (Praha, Melantrich, 1947). The principal Engliš theses may be traced, however, throughout all his principal writings.

11. He published the results in 1925 in German in his *Grundlagen des wirtschaftlichen Denkens*. At that time Engliš' theoretical analysis was chiefly directed at German economists such as R. Liefmann, K. Diehl, H. Dietzel, Fr. Oppenheimer, etc., for whom methodology in economics was a primary issue. For other Engliš' writings concerning logic in economics, see the Appendix.

12. See especially his *Základy hospodářskeho myšlení* (= *Sbírka spisů právních a národohospodářských*, Sv. 21) (Praha, 1922) pp. 38 ff.; *cf.* also Engliš' criticism of Liefmann's theories.

13. Englis acknowledges Richert's influence in *Teleogie*, p. 11

14. Ibid., pp. 12-14

15. Ibid., pp. 22 ff.

16. Engliš recognizes still another non-ontological scientific approach, that is, normology, used in the normative science of law. In effect, he acknowledges his great indebtness to his colleague, Professor F. Weyr, and also to Professor Hans Kelsen, whose ideas about a normative theory of law provided Engliš with the necessary stimulus in his search for a method peculiar to economic analysis (Cf., *Soustava*, p. XI). The relationship of normology to teleology is, however, beyond the scope of this Introduction. It may suffice to mention merely that Engliš believed that normative sciences are, in a way, a subgroup in the larger teleologically ordered systems and that teleological stage precedes the normative explanation in law. Thus in ibid., pp. 72-78. On the somewhat different attitude of the exponents of the normative theory of law, see František Weyr, *Teorie Práva* (Brno, Orbis, 1936); Hans Kelsen, *General Theory of Law and State* (Cambridge, Massachusetts, Harvard University Press, 1949); and Adolph Procházka, "Normativní teorie a tvorba práva", *Sborník Prací k Padesátým Narozeninám Karla Engliše*, ed. F. Weyr (Praha, Orbis, 1930), pp. 436-455. In the same publication is an article by Vladimír Vybral, a Professor of Public Finance at Masaryk University, giving an excellent review of the background to Engliš' theories; see "Problematika principu hospodárnosti v hospodářské teorii," *Sborník*, pp. 93-143.

17. *Hodocení*, pp. 29-44; *Teleologie,* pp. 29 ff. Of course, there are branches of economics as, e.g., economic history, economic statistics, etc. in which the "executed" purposes are the subject of analysis. Here the cause-effect principle is appropriately used. But for theoretical, anticipative cognition of economic behavior, only the teleological approach is practical. It should also be mentioned that Engliš strongly rejects any suggestion, as found in Kant and Wundt, that the *nexus finalis* is simply a reversed *nexus effectivus.* Engliš' arguments are involved and too lengthy to be examined here but may be found in *Soustava,* pp. 6-13, and namely in his *Apologia finalitatis; rosprava o Tardym* (Praha, Knohovna Sborníku věd Právních a Státních, 1947).

18. *Hodnocení*, pp. 64-67.

19. Their best presentation can be found in Engliš' *Hospodárské soustavy* (Praha, Všehrd, 1946), p. 66b, hereinafter quoted as *Soustavy,* 1946.

20. *Soustava,* pp. 25-34

21. Ibid., pp. 34, 52-53; compared with this "a personal solidarity of purposes" which characterizes a system in which all persons, i.e., a nation, are the object of care under the primary purpose set up by a state.

22. Ibid., pp. 55-57

23. The most illuminating analysis of purposive (i.e., teleological) organizations can be found in Ludwigs von Bertalanffy: *General System Theory: Foundations, Development, Applications.* New York, George Braziller, 1968; especially 16-29; 37-41; 45-49; 91-92.

24. Note some recent efforts to formulate a new index of economic welfare more meaningful than GNP. This is discussed briefly below.

25. Bertalanffy, *op. cit.,* pp. 75 ff.

26. In my previous writings on K. Engliš, I used the term "organic utility of purposes" with reference to Engliš' solidaristic nexus. However, as "organic" is a biological rather than economic term, I rethought the entire part of Engliš' discussions of the nexus relationships. I believe that as presented here, it more closely reflects his ideas.

27. Bertalanffy, *op. cit.,* pp. 56 ff, and notably equation 3.1.

28. According to a personal communication from Prof. Ivo Moravčík.

29. Note also that system theory rejects a suggestion by some that teleological methodology is nothing but reverse causality, a point rejected by K. Engliš long time ago; see, for instance, *Apologia Finalitatis . . . ,* quoted in appended Bibliography.

30. In this respect Engliš' ideas are akin to those of Walter Eucken, who emphasized the significance of the relationship between economic, social and political structures in his search for a generalized logical model of *Wirtschaftsysteme.See* his *Die Grundlagen der Nationaloekonomie,* Jena 1940. Cf., also works of François Perroux and Johann Akerman, who among other Continental economists, pursued similar thoughts during that period.

31. Paul Samuelson, *Economics.* Ninth Edition. New York: McGraw Hill Co., 1973; pp. 1 ff; Ch. 42 "Winds of Change: Evolution of Economic Doctrines," and Ch. 43 "Alternative Economic Systems."

32. E.g., Joe S. Bain, *Price Theory.* New York: Henry Holt and Company, 1952; pp. 1 ff, especially p. 4.

33. See his *Welfare Economics and the Theory of the State.* 2nd Ed. Cambridge: Harvard University Press, 1965; pp. 36-47 and quoted literature there; also Ch. 12, especially pp. 192-96.

34. See footnotes (16) and (17).

35. Cf. his critical "Comments on the Papers by Daly and Stiglitz" in *Scarcity and Growth Reconsidered.* Kerry V. Smith, Ed., Baltimore and London: The Johns Hopkins University Press, 1979, pp. 95-105, and other of his writings quoted there.

36. Published for Resources for the Future, Inc. by Johns Hopkins Press, Baltimore 1958. This clearly teleologically conceptualized economic model has earned an international recognition and was used for various natural resource projects throughout the world. See also Krutilla's *The Columbia River Treaty: The Economics of an International River Development.* Baltimore: the Johns Hopkins Press, 1967.

37. Cf., his *Wealth and Welfare: Collected Essays on Economic Theory.* Vol. 1. Cambridge: Harvard University Press, 1981; Part I, 1; pp. 3-55.

38. 370 US 469; see also *Philadelphia National Bank* case, 374 US 321; or *Proctor and Gamble Co.,* 358 F.2d74 (6th Circ.), which among others were decided along the lines of the *Brown Shoe Co.* case.

39. This is obvious from the numerous translations of Engliš' writings into a number of European languages other than English, but notably into German. See the Bibliography and especially the Addendum.

40. Lewis H. Haney, *History of Economic Thought.* New York: McMillan Co., 1949, p. 819, where K. Engliš is placed in the Austrian School among Schumpeter, Wieser, Mises, Hayek, Philipovitch and others.

I. FOREWORD

An economic system is an order whereby a nation exercises care to maintain and improve its life. The term "nation" is used here in its political sense; it refers to the population of a given state's territory governed by a sovereign central authority. The central authority either exercises care to maintain and improve the nation's life directly, or else sanctions whatever order arises spontaneously, possibly only regulating the latter within certain limits. When I say, "a nation exercises care", I mean by that that the nation has established some system of economic care (to maintain and improve its life) and that it performs this function within such framework–whether each individual assumes responsibility for his own welfare, or whether the central authority is responsible for the welfare of all.

This study is concerned with a specific advanced stage of economic development in which the modern political state has attained maturity and assumed the function of regulating the nation's economic problems. I am not concerned with the stage of a closed, in natura economy, nor other older, decentralized economies. In any event, what I say about the national economy holds analogously for such decentralized economies within a state (e.g., the city economy as Bucher uses the term).

By "economic system" I understand that which is referred to as individualism, capitalism, socialism, cooperation, communism, solidarism, etc. Many volumes have been devoted to this subject but they are not satisfactory.

1. The essence of socialism, communism, solidarism, etc., as systems opposed to individualism or capitalism, has not been brought out. The opposition of private (individual) ownership and social or collective (state)* ownership, has generally been stressed. However, concentration of ownership (control of goods) in the hands of the state does not define, without ambiguity, the specific order of care exercised by the state to maintain and improve the nation's life. When the state nationalizes an industry, e.g., the manufacture of footwear, this does not, itself, imply a particular system of production. The state may continue to manufacture shoes in the same way as was done by Bata**, i.e., to produce such quantities and qualities of shoes as the public prefers and is willing to buy, so as to maximize profit via such production (state capitalism). Alternatively, the state may continue to produce such footwear as the public prefers and wants to buy, but for the sole purpose of serving the public's subjective wants, rather than for profit which is excluded in this case (state cooperation). Finally, the state may produce only such footwear that it views as objectively useful, both to the nation and to the individual, (from the viewpoint of its purpose—as a father for his children) and to allocate shoes to the public without payment, seeking compensation in the people's contribution based on their ability to contribute (solidarism).

Control of goods (ownership) represents only one lever of the systemic apparatus. The same type of state control of goods may characterize different systems which are not adequately described in terms of such control. In any case, no socialist has ever logically and consistently worked out the system of a socialist state. In particular, no such positive exposition was presented by Marx.

2. The situation is no different when socialism is described in terms of guaranteeing the right to work or the right to a living (A. Menger), particularly when these are seen merely as variants of the same thing. The right to work and the right to a living characterize different economic

———

* Alternatively, a distinction is made between ownership of various types of consumer and producer goods. (K. Diehl)

** Translator's Note: A large private enterprise in pre-Communist Czechoslovakia whose major product was footwear.

systems, and their consistent realization could not take place within the same system. We shall see that the right to work characterizes the national cooperation, while the right to a living characterizes solidarism. A particular order must be understood as an integral whole, a genuine system of coherent, order-determined elements; it cannot be described only in terms of a specific lever of the systemic apparatus.

3. Naturally, when a systemic order is not properly understood, when it is only described in terms of one of its elements, one cannot gain a systematic understanding of different economic systems, i.e., an exposition that would be clearly complete and would logically exhaust all alternatives. More than that cannot be done! Such exposition would show the nature of a system's logical internal structure; what constitutes the basis of the alternatives. It would also make possible a correct classification of different economic systems. When we inquire why the science of economics has failed in this task, we discover its logical-noetic confusion. An economic system, can only be understood by means of the teleological system of cognition. But the science of economics, notwithstanding the fact that it operates with concepts such as utility, good, cost, ends, means, etc., has nevertheless always endeavored to be a causal science, and as a result has suffered from logical-noetic confusion. It has failed to realize that when we view activities and objects as desired by someone, objects forthwith become goods, activities useful or detrimental, everything a means or an end. Economics has failed to realize that in maximizing an end, action follows the principle of economizing in accordance with relative utilities and costs, up to the margin of rationality, etc. Economic activity is end-oriented. It represents an order which cannot be understood as a system, except by the teleological system of cognition. When one uses the ontological-causal approach, conceiving of everything as simply existing, as cause and effect, then order disappears; goods, utility, loss, return, etc., vanish; indeed the agent himself vanishes.

It was precisely the teleological approach which enabled me to present an exposition of economic systems free of the shortcomings of other expositions. A comprehensive presentation of the teleological system of cognition appeared in my works on logic.* It is the foundation of the

---

* *Malá logika Věda o myšlenkovém řádu [Compact Logic: The Science of the System of Thinking]*, Prague, Melantrich, 1946. *Die Lehre von der Denkordnung,* Wien, Rohrer Verlag, 1961.

whole of my economic theory (*Soustava narodniho hospodarstvi [System of National Economy*] 1938).

Exposition of economic systems is the foundation of all other fields of economics. When one asks, e.g., what is economic value, one cannot give an answer applicable to other than a specific economic system, because—as we shall see—economic value differs as between systems.

Except for minor corrections and additions, the present study was written during the last year of the war, to facilitate the understanding of ideas and movements that were certain to make their appearance once the war was over.

Prague, October 1945
Dr. Karel Engliš

II. THE POLARITY OF ECONOMIC SYSTEMS

Only two alternatives are possible: (a) every individual looks after his own welfare, he is the agent exercising care for himself, or (b) each individual, and the nation, are objects of the care of another, the care-exercising agent being someone else, such as when a father provides for his children, or when the state exercises care for its people.

Any care for human welfare, in each of the above cases, has as its purpose that which the agent wishes to achieve by exercising such care. In principle, however, the ends in the two cases are different.

Ad (a): When an individual is responsible for his own welfare, when he is the agent who provides for himself, then each active expression of his care, and such care in its totality, are directed toward his satisfaction, his freedom from pain, the maximization of his pleasure. In that case the end of personal satisfaction is subjective and substantively non-communicable. It is not possible to make generally valid (objective) statements about that which is desired, in each specific instance, to yield individual satisfaction. Only the individual himself can make such statements. When an object or an activity contribute to his subjective satisfaction he attributes to them subjective utility, assigns to them positive subjective value. In case of diminution of satisfaction, pain, there is subjective disutility and negative subjective value. All the actions of the individual—though he may pursue a great variety of ends—appear as an ordered complex whose apex is the subjective end of personal satisfaction—the ordering principle. From this end are derived subjective wants (for means to increase personal satisfaction), subjective goods (objects wanted for the same purpose), subjective utilities and values (utility represents realization of the end, disutility is a diminution of utility, value is the measure and degree of utility), etc. The use of resources within this complex of a subjective economic unit occurs in accordance with diminishing relative utility per resource unit, while resources are obtained (produced) at increasing relative costs. The process continues until the point is reached where relative utility no longer exceeds relative cost, where the two are equal. At this point is the boundary of rationality, the limit of the rational process, the margin of producing goods, and the cause of their general scarcity.* (See graph on p. 32.)

In this way man satisfies his various wants (food, clothing, culture, etc.) according to his personal objectives, his subjective utilities and costs. The following question arises: How far does he proceed in satisfying different wants? Given the scarcity of resources (determined by the limit of rationality) it is clear that, while satisfying one want, the individual must not neglect the fact that he has other wants. Otherwise he could satisfy one want fully, deriving very little utility at the margin, while neglecting another altogether, thus foregoing much higher potential utility. In satisfying a particular want, he must not proceed any further if satisfaction of another promises to yield higher relative utility per resource unit (labor unit, unit of money). This implies equalization of relative marginal utilities among various wants (incremental utilities derived from satisfaction of various wants). There exists therefore within this, or any other economic unit a *nexus of material solidarity* between the different wants that are satisfied, as distinct from the nexus of *personal solidarity* about which more will be said later. This is the balance of satisfaction of different wants within a given economic unit which was already sought (in vain) by Gossen. Such balance implies neither equality of resources employed nor of the wants satisfied (utilities derived), nor of the wants that are not satisfied (utilities foregone), but rather equality of relative marginal utilities. We shall see, that personal solidarity also implies a kind of balance. It is because of this nexus of wants that the economic unit is an integral whole, an order.

---

* A special, less distant, boundary may exist when a good is non-repordducible (unique goods, etc.).

A specific intermediate end (food, shelter, books) may be objective (its content may be communicated), but all such specific (technical) ends converge in a central and ultimate end which is primary, cannot be ordered any further and is subjective (its content cannot be communicated). The teleological explanation of an individual's care for his own welfare is subjectivist because the purpose of the order is subjective welfare.

Ad (b): When the care-exercising agent and the object of care are distinct (the individual is cared for by someone else) the situation becomes fundamentally different. To understand such care one must search for its purpose, for that which the agent wishes to accomplish, at the apex of the complex of activities of which such care consists. The first purpose that governs such complex is some state of the object of care. One desires that the individual who is the object of one's care should live, be healthy, that he should be cultured (by which we mean certain moral and intellectual qualities). In short, this represents a particular educational ideal. We say that this is the "first" purpose governing the complex, because there may be other, more distant ends, i.e., something that one wishes to attain through the individual's acquisition of the qualities of the educational ideal. E.g., one may believe that the individual will then be happy; or the care-exercising agent may prefer certain specific qualities, etc. However, such more distant ends are not needed to explain the exercise of care as a specific complex, if one has already derived by discovering the first purpose—the expositional and ordering center of the entire complex (but that complex alone). Proceeding toward higher ends changes (expands) the complex. E.g., if one considers a distant end, as when the agent (the father) desires happiness of the object of his care (the child), one explains not only such care but other actions of the agent (the father) as well. For instance, he may be accumulating, for this reason, an estate for his children. If one proceeds all the way to the subjective end of the care-exercising agent who prefers a particular kind of care one actually explains all of the agent's actions that lead to his subjective end, not only the exercise of care as such. Thus when an absolute ruler exercises care for a nation in a specific manner, and we inquire as to the purpose of such care, we cannot go all the way to his subjective end (he prefers it that way), because we are not interested in explaining all that the ruler (as a man) does but only in explaining the specific complex of his actions that we interpret in terms of the end that covers only this complex. And that is a specific educational ideal.

What holds for men holds analogously for the care of animals. When one cares for dogs, one's purpose is to breed a qualitatively ideal type of dog—as envisioned by the care-exercising agent—through cross-breeding, feeding, or training. Care for man too need not start at birth; one may go further (eugenics), and this is rational, since some qualities, inherited, cannot be attained through post-natal care.

From the standpoint of logic such end is objective because its content may be communicated, and anyone can make a generally valid value judgment about what he likes or dislikes, what gives him utility (an increase in the attainment of his end), and what causes him disutility (a decrease in the attainment of his end). From the objective end follow objective need, utility, disutility, value, etc. Hence all considerations of care for an individual by a person other than himself are objective, they can be subject to control and criticism.

However, we are concerned here not only with the case of an individual as an object of someone else's care, but with the case of an entire nation as the object of such care. After all, we are concerned with the order by which a nation exercises care to maintain and improves its life. Here the question becomes more complicated. Complexity arises even in formulating the purpose of care as an ordering principle. In the case of care for an individual the question is merely that of listing his qualities in some harmonious balance. But when a whole nation is involved then all the qualities of all its members cannot be the same: There exist natural differences of age, those that are inherited, etc. Hence the ideal of care must also include the ideal of a nation's development corresponding to such differences, i.e., its development with respect to age, sex, etc. E.g., a given age structure represented by a pyramid shows base corners that represent children who will not live to productive ages; they are a burden on the nation (fathers, mothers, society). They will die before they can return anything to society, before they can help to provide for others. The ideal is a prism in which each member of a lower stratum progresses all the way to the highest level, so that the body dies off only at the top, and any widening of the base signifies a population increase. The ideal includes as well the quantitative ideal of population size: One seeks an optimal relationship between the quality, the size of the population,etc.

Thus in seeking to derive maximum utility from consuming a particular good, one must consider not only ideal educational qualities but also who will receive the good. In producing and consuming goods it is important not only whether additional food or more books yield more utility, but also who receives what. For the hungry food is of greater importance than books because the first concern of the hungry is to preserve life, while the converse holds for the satiated.

If the care-exercising agent is to provide for the nation in accordance with this purpose he will have to allocate labor not only to the production of various goods, but to assign it to individual members of the community. In distributing goods he will have to consider not only various subordinate ends, different wants (aspects of the ideal of care), but also the different individuals. As we saw in the case of an individual exercising care for his own welfare, allocation of resources to various wants, to subordinate ends, results in a nexus among these wants, a nexus of material solidarity. But objective care for a nation, guided by the ideal of the nation's life, health, and culture, considers not only the spectrum of wants emerging from this end. It not only stands in their midst, facing the nexus of their material solidarity, but must also consider individual members of the community among whom are allocated both the burdens and the fruits of labor. Here too the first aspect leads to a nexus between various wants (aspects of the ideal), i.e., a nexus of material solidarity. However, the second aspect implies, over and above that, a particular nexus of personal solidarity among individual members of the community.

This is so because more utility will be derived from providing medicine to the sick than to the healthy, or from giving a book to the less educated than to those better supplied with books. Helping the weak, saving their lives, yields more utility than a surfeit of culture for others. "More utility" refers here to the view of the care-exercising agent (e.g., the state) and to his purpose. The state derives utility from curing the sick, a benefit resulting from its active exercise of care. It represents therefore an objective benefit rather than subjective utility of the individual who is the object of care. The latter (subjective utility) cannot be valued by the care-exercising agent (the state) who can only value objective utility. If we refer, even in this case, to the needs of the object of care, e.g., if we say that "the patient needs quiet", we do not mean his *active*, subjective want, but his *passive* need, that corresponds to the active want of the care-exercising agent (the state). If we say that a person who has lost consciousness needs smelling salts, or that an infant needs to be vacincated, we clearly do not refer to *subjective* want of the unconscious person or the infant, but rather to the active, *objective* want of the care-exercising agent who desires that the unconscious should live and that the sick should become healthy, and who therefore desires also the appropriate means. The situation is analogous to that of a farmer who says that his cattle need to be fed or the housewife who says that the soup needs more salt. To the extent that the objective desire of the care-exercising agent is projected to the object of care and we speak of the latter's need, what we mean is his *passive* need, a corollary of the active desire of the care-exercising agent. In this case, when we say, e.g., that goods are distributed among citizens according to their needs, we do not mean that they are distributed according to their subjective wants, in accordance with their desires, but rather according to the objective desires of the care-exercising agent (the state) and in accordance with "how needy they are found to be".

Accordingly one cannot use a good for the benefit of an individual if the relative utility derived from using it for the benefit of another is greater. Similarly one cannot assign the burden of labor to an individual if the cost, the resulting objective loss relative to the ideal of care, is less in the case of another individual. Otherwise one would fail to maximize the attainment of the end. But this implies equalization of relative utilities and costs among different individuals who are once again found to be in a nexus of utility-and-cost solidarity. But this is *personal* solidarity, as distinct from the *material* solidarity that exists among different wants. Naturally, such personal solidarity does not exist when individuals are responsible for their own welfare. Personal solidarity thus characterizes the care for a nation where the latter is the object of care directed toward the ideal of life, health, and culture.

What is the meaning of the equalization of marginal utilities among individuals, of personal solidarity? It does not mean equality of consumption among members of the community, since goods are distributed according to relative utilities (more to the economically weaker, less to the economically stronger). Nor does it mean equal burdens of labor expended in the provision of means because labor is assigned on the basis of relative costs, on the basis of capacity to work (more to the stronger, less to the weaker). Once again we have here a type of balance. But it is now derived from the purpose, the endeavor to attain the ideal of life, health, and culture for the nation as a whole. Hence the effort to achieve, among individuals, a balance of those qualities that make up the ideal of care: A balanced development of the citizens toward the ideal of life, health, and culture.

To each of the above two cases corresponds a particular economic order or system of care to maintain and improve the nation's life. Hence the polarity of economic systems consists of the following:

(a) In the first case the individual is the agent exercising care for his own welfare, whereas in the second case both the individual and the nation are objects of someone else's care.

(b) In the first case the ruling and ordering purpose is the individual's personal satisfaction—which is subjective—whereas in the second case the ruling and ordering purpose is the ideal of the nation's life, health, and culture—which is objective.

(c) The first case of exercising care is characterized by a nexus of material solidarity of wants, whereas in the second case there is also, in addition to this, a nexus of personal solidarity among members of the community.

We refer to systems of the first type as individualistic because their point of departure is the individual exercising care for his own welfare. We refer to the system of the second type as solidaristic, in view of the relationship of personal solidarity among members of the community. The solidarist system is the logical counterpart of individualistic systems (we say *systems* because there are two such systems).

III. INDIVIDUALISTIC SYSTEMS: CAPITALISM AND NATIONAL COOPERATION

1. Introduction

Individualistic systems have the following features in common: The individual is the starting point of the exercise of care for maintaining and improving the nation's life, and hence of the system of such care. The individual is responsible for his own welfare, in accordance with his subjective valuation. Consequently in these systems both the volume and the structure of production and consumption, the point to which production and consumption of various goods is carried, are determined by subjective valuation. To put it negatively, it can be also said that from the standpoint of the nation—how the nation derives more or less utility by producing and consuming—no objective valuation exists (as distinct from the care exercised in solidarism).

When we speak nevertheless of an order (system) of care for maintaining and improving the nation's life, the order cannot have its basis in a single specific purpose, as is the case in an homogeneously solidarist economy for the nation as a whole, because there is no such homogeneity here. After all, each individual exercises care for himself and determines his various wants in accordance with his subjective valuation. Nevertheless, we speak of an order (system) of *national* care, even in this case, because certain common institutions for the balance of production and consumption, as well as other balances, emerge in the care for the nation. What we have here, therefore, is an equilibrium system which is secondary, as distinct from the order deriving directly from a specific purpose, as in the case of a single individual economic unit, or an economy which is homogeneously solidarist for the whole nation.

The distinction between individualistic systems is to be found in the nature of common institutions that serve the nation's care for maintaining and improving its life and were created for the purpose of equilibrium. This includes:

1. *How* such institutions were formed; and
2. *What* institutions were thus formed.

Ad 1: Here the decisive distinction is between spontaneity and voluntariness on one hand, versus planning and compulsion on the other. Only those institutions can emerge spontaneously and voluntarily that are in harmony with the interests of individual economic units seeking mutual relationships. Planning and compulsion lead to the creation of other institutions.

Ad 2: Hence the question of what institutions are created for the purpose of an equilibrium order, relates to the question of how institutions are created, whether spontaneously, voluntarily or through planning and compulsion. In this respect, as we shall see, the two individualistic systems depart from each other. National cooperation is a negation of and stands opposed to capitalism.

2. The Capitalist System

Exchange (of one good for another, etc.) is at the basis of capitalist institutions, which arise spontaneously from interests of individual economic units and tend toward an equilibrium order of care for maintaining and improving the nation's life. Exchange derives from the interests of both (all) participating parties; they derive utility from it, because it yields to each something from which he obtains–according to his valuation–more utility in exchange for something which–again according to his valuation–promises less utility. Exchange therefore raises the utility level of the participants. It leads to division of labor which raises productivity and is made possible by utility-augmenting exchange. It leads to introduction of money which facilitates exchange. Hence capitalist money always represents either some quantity of a good or some quantity, set, of all goods (purchasing power). A market for goods comes into being.

As the use of money becomes universal it breaks up the original, complete, and self-sufficient individual economic unit, which produces all that it needs, and consumes all that it produces, into two separate sectors, namely the household sector and the business sector (enterprises). The criterion of the division is the relation to money. The entire national economy is divided into two sectors: on one side of the market are households (the household sector); on the other are enterprises (the business sector). Enterprises make money, they generate incomes for those who participate in their activity. The earnings flow to the household sector where they are used to purchase consumer goods. Enterprises make money by supplying, directly or indirectly, goods and services to the household sector, by selling goods to consumers.

Not everyone can start his own business; those who cannot, work for wages in enterprises that belong to others. The working class comes into being, and the labor market emerges, where those offering their labor for wages meet those offering employment. A capital market is also formed, on the basis of savings from income and liquid capital funds of enterprises (from sales of assets, from decreased production or trade). Finally, there also comes into being the foreign exchange market, where instruments for foreign payments are bought and sold, which involves international relations.

Each market is an equilibrating mechanism, and the only law of price formation is the principle of equilibrium. Price, in a broad sense, includes the price of goods, the price of labor (the wage rate), and the price of money (the interest rate). Prices of goods bring about balance between production and consumption; the price of labor balances supply and demand for labor; and the price of money (the interest rate) balances supply and demand for capital funds. Supply and demand are not the law of price formation, because price is one of the determinants of both supply and demand. Nor are prices determined by production costs, because different producers have different costs, and because so-called marginal costs, which determine market supply, are themselves price-determined, the quantities of goods required to supply the market being dependent on their prices. Prices of all goods figure in the calculations of consumers, whose behavior as buyers depends on the relative utility of the money unit (as prices fall relative utilities rise). Prices also figure in the calculations of producers, whose behavior depends upon the relative costs of earning a unit of money. In this way are formed ratios of prices of various goods. Price ratios are the inverse of exchange ratios. For example, if one kilo of meat sells for five units of money and one kilo of flour for one unit of money, the amount of flour that exchanges for a given amount of meat is five times larger. Relative prices may remain unchanged even when the price level changes as the value of a unit of money changes (inflation, deflation, devaluation, etc.).

Prices in all markets are inter-related. E.g., if interest rates rise, entrepreneurs find that it does not pay to continue producing a given output at existing prices and wages (profits may be eroded or losses occur). Enterprises would liquidate inventories and lay off workers. In this way entrepreneurs (or rather the rate of interest) exercise downward pressure on wage rates and prices. Conversely, a change in the price level affects interest rates and wage rates, while a change in the wage level affects prices and interest rates. There can therefore be no equilibrium in one market unless there is equilibrium in all markets, because disequilibrium in one market spills over into other markets. This also applies to the foreign exchange market. Thus capitalism emerges as an equilibrium economic order, associated with three types of equilibria in the domestic market and one in the market for instruments of foreign payments. Nobody establishes or maintains this order through planning. It arises spontaneously as a by-product of market relationships. The state, as sovereign authority, does not control the nation's care for maintaining and improving its life. It merely protects, negatively, various acquired rights and the observance of contractual obligations. All individual economic units are thus inter-related, each depends on all others, because their decisions are based on prices. Each depends on the whole, and the whole depends on each of them. We are therefore justified in saying that this is an order in which the nation exercises care for maintaining and improving its life.

Consumption in capitalism depends on incomes received by individuals as participants in business activity. It is thus a function of the earnings of enterprises as "working teams" whose participants include entrepreneurs who organize enterprises on their own account, capitalists who lend them money at interest, and the employees, workers who sell labor power to enterprises for wages. The balance of value added by such working team is derived from the value of goods produced, or sold, less the value of goods devoted to production, both the goods used up, such as lumber or paint, and those not used up (depreciation of machinery or structures). Such balance of value added forms the objective return of the enterprise as a working team. All the participants–the entrepreneur, the worker, and the capitalist–have contributed to it. This return, which is divided among the participants, is the source of their incomes and their consumption expenditures and the basis of their existence.

How is the division effected? This too depends on prices, the price of money (the rate of interest) and the price of labor (the wage rate). Equilibrium prices thus form the key for division of objective enterprise returns into income shares of the participants. The aggregate of the objective returns of all enterprises is the return of national economic activity and, since it is the only source from which incomes are derived, it constitutes the national income. Shares in the return of national economic activity received by entrepreneurs, workers, and capitalists are not expressions of an objective contribution, of what particular individuals had contributed to enterprise returns. They are rather an outcome of the equilibrating process in the market.

A change in the principle of price formation occurs in later stages of capitalist development. In place of competition leading to equilibrium market prices, economic units on either side of the market enter into price agreements. When this occurs, price is no longer an equilibrium price, and equilibrium must be negotiated. Such agreements are negotiated to arrive at a price different from the competitive price, because it is more advantageous for the economic units that are parties to such agreements. If such non-competitive price is to persist, there must be permanent agreements and organizations–*cartels.* When there are too many dispersed economic units, e.g., in the household sector, or when vested interests are only temporary–e.g., those of debtors–cartellization does not occur. Conversely, where vested interests are permanent, concurrent, and affecting the existence of the economic units, conditions for cartellization exist. There are producers' cartels in the market for goods, cartels of financial institutions in the money market, syndicates of employers and of employees in the labor market. Syndicates are known as trade unions or industry associations because both workers and producers tend to organize syndicates in trades or industries where there would be competition: A steel worker does not compete with a textile worker.

The displacement of price by cartels requires that equilibrium in a given market be artificially established, to correspond to the administered price. Otherwise the administered price could not persist, and cartels would break down. This leads to establishment of production quotas and re-allocation of production within the cartel. In the labor market appear collective agreements for entire industries, or wage-classification agreements containing general rules for negotiating individual agreements (hiring procedures).

Why is the system known as capitalism? The term is derived from "capital", i.e., all the assets used in production, especially by enterprises. Capital must have priority in receiving its share—interest. Otherwise investment would vanish, and existing investments would be liquidated along with enterprises. The life of the enterprise is closely associated with the priority share of capital in the objective return of the enterprise as a working team. Capitalism is an entrepreneurial system of production.

Enterprises, or shares in enterprises, shares of capital stock, can be controlled either by individuals or by the state. In the latter case they do not cease to be enterprises, provided they are managed with profit maximization as their objective. In that case we speak of *state capitalism*. The state performs the entrepreneurial function alongside individuals and corporations. Because it engages in entrepreneurial activity as a profit-seeking agent similar to a corporation, nothing is changed in the entrepreneurial economic system, except that profit accrues to the state and hence society as a whole. Profit becomes a source of state revenue, in addition to taxes and other payments. State capitalism is not a distinct economic system. Indeed, it would not be a separate system even if all entrepreneurial activity were conducted by the state. However, it would then become pointless for the state to make money in this manner, to receive all entrepreneurial income. The state would not need such income, unless it was simultaneously a *solidarist* state with revenue derived from enterprise profits rather than taxes. But this would contradict the state's solidarist end of production based on capacity to contribute. On the other hand, if the state were not the recipient of the revenues of enterprises under its control, then the enterprises would be transformed into national cooperatives. State capitalism is thus conceivable only within the framework and as a sector of private capitalism.

A state enterprise, even if not as yet transformed into a cooperative, may not only be a source of income of the solidarist economy, but may also operate within the solidarist purpose of serving customers better, selling to them at lower prices, or treating workers better, paying them higher wages and requiring shorter hours than private enterprises. This would be at the expense of entrepreneurial profit, though profit would still exist. Such enterprise would be known as a public enterprise, though not yet a cooperative.

For the employees, the mere transfer of an enterprise to the state, or some other public body, with no change in the economic order, does have some moral significance. The point is that workers do not see the purpose of their labor only in the light of their earnings, but also from the standpoint of who is served and what purpose is served by their labor. In a war of national defense workers are motivated to better performance, not only by the prospect of compensation, wages, but also by awareness of making a contribution to their country's defense. Of course, this applies as well to private enterprises engaged in defense production. We must therefore distinguish the objective of making money from other ends of labor which can be brought together under the heading "the mission of labor". This includes e.g. the question of whom labor serves and what need it serves. Enlightened entrepreneurs also view the meaning of their work and the activity of their enterprises in this way, not only as a way of making money, but as a means of providing a livelihood for their workers, improving a community or a region, and providing, by means of their products, better nutrition, clothing, footwear, medical care, less heavy labor (use of machinery), etc., to a wide circle of customers, to all those who demand these things.

Workers may also view their labor from this viewpoint. On the other hand, they may view it as service rendered to private entrepreneurs, whom they help to earn profits and increase wealth (capital). Such a view is especially appropriate when the entrepreneurs consider their activities as having no other purpose than to make money. This in turn tends to be the case when there is no "personal" entrepreneur, but only share capital, whose owners have no interest in the enterprise other than to make money.

When the state takes over an enterprise there is no material change as far as either the public or the workers are concerned. The state enterprise does not become publicly controlled, let alone cooperative. Nevertheless, the workers' moral view of the purpose of their labor, other than wages, does change. They come to view their role as no longer serving private interests of capitalists, but rather those of the whole. Of course, this depends on the *political* structure of the state, as well as the workers' moral values.

And so, even though takeover of enterprises by the state, state capitalism, is not an economic system distinct from capitalism, it does introduce a new moral and psychological element. Of course if state capitalism were to take over most or all production formerly carried on by private enterprises, it could not remain, economically, a capitalist system, and would inevitably drift either toward national cooperation or solidarism.

3. The Cooperative System

Growth of private enterprise is accompanied by the growth of the class of employees and workers whose livelihood depends on wages. They observe that their share of national income consists of wages, but they view the national product, the material basis of national income, as created, from the bounty of mother nature, by labor alone. And yet a considerable share is claimed by entrepreneurs as profits and capitalists as interest. The workers believe that this is unjust, since such incomes are not received "for work" or "productive contribution". In their view, labor alone represents a just principle of distribution of national product and income. Furthermore, disturbances in the operation of the capitalist economy (depressions) cause unemployment, which means that propertyless workers (the proletariat—those who leave behind only *proles,* i.e., offspring, but no wealth) lose the only basis of their livelihood. This critique leads to the following demands of labor:

1. Non-labor incomes, profit and interest, should be abolished, and labor should become the only basis for income distribution. The "right to the undiminished proceeds of labor" should be put into effect.

2. Since work is, generally, labor's only source of income, everyone should be endowed with the "right to work".

This critique leads to efforts to replace business enterprise and its functions by some alternative. In performing its function, business serves those to whom it sells goods and services, especially consumers, and those from whom it buys finished products (trading enterprises), as well as raw materials and intermediate goods, (e.g., steel mills).* Business also serves those whom it employs, primarily workers, by contributing to the earning of their incomes. Those for whom business enterprises thus perform such services tend to associate themselves for the purpose of replacing the services of business enterprises by cooperation. Such associations are known as *cooperatives.* Depending on the functions of the enterprises which they replace, there are consumers' cooperatives (for the purpose of joint purchases), marketing cooperatives (for joint marketing of grain, milk, etc.), and producers' cooperatives for joint production carried on without entrepreneurs (workers' production cooperatives). Some writers believe that cooperation is the way to solve the whole social problem (Louis Blanc), while others want to base the "new society" on cooperatives (Hertzka: *Freiland*). However, historical experience has shown that when cooperatives have operated alongside business enterprises, they have failed to abolish interest, the money market, and capital (and hence income from capital). They succeeded only in abolishing entrepreneurial profit (for themselves), but this was insufficient to eliminate competing business enterprises.

The next step involves the assumption of the cooperative function by *public bodies:* municipalities, districts, provinces, the state. As noted above, these bodies also operate enterprises. But, when they assume the function of cooperatives, they come to serve all citizens as cooperatives serve their members, without striving to maximize profits. Former business enterprises may thus be transformed into cooperatives by abandoning the pursuit of profit, e.g., by lowering prices or improving workers' conditions. It is in this manner that municipalities provide water, electricity, public baths, transportation, and other services to citizens. We speak here of public cooperation or better still the cooperative function of public bodies, the real foundation of such undertakings. The payments to public bodies for cooperatively supplied goods and services are called *fees*, which are thus cooperative prices. Cooperative undertakings

---

* so-called "key production."

of public bodies tend to replace business enterprise only in certain areas such as municipal public transport or local water systems. However, they do not replace business enterprise in general and hence abolish neither interest nor entrepreneurial income. Such partial cooperation, whether non-governmental or operated by public bodies, is also unable to bring about realization of the right to work. These objectives would be almost completely attained in a system of *national cooperation* in which the state would take over the operation of all enterprises and run them on the same basis as they are run under partial cooperation. It would produce what the public demanded, as much of each good as was demanded. But the prices charged would not include profit. All goods and services would sell at prices that covered only cost.

Consuming economic units would survive but private business enterprise would disappear. Its activity would be carried on by state establishments, the technical counterpart of business enterprises. Since the money market and interest are largely a creation of the business sector (compared to business credit, consumers' credit is negligible), income from capital would disappear, and the only income of consumers would be income earned by work in state establishments. Since no other income would exist, everyone would have to have the right to work and we shall see that it would be possible for everyone to enjoy this right. Consumers would use their income to make purchases in state stores according to their subjective valuations, the subjective relative utility of the work unit. Everyone would receive income for his work and be responsible for his own welfare. Since the state would produce goods in such quantities as the public bought, production would be guided by subjective valuations. In accordance with these two aspects, the pure cooperative system should be classified as part of the individualistic order, despite the collectivist nature of cooperative production.

Subjective valuation in the cooperative system is constrained by income from work and the available stock of goods in stores, because the amount of income units in circulation equals the value of goods in the stores. Purchases reduce incomes paid out and the stock of goods in stores by equal amounts, so that there is balance between the two. Of course, this is so only because the work unit is used as cost unit, price unit, and income unit. If an individual performs ten work units producing a particular product, he receives an income of ten units, and the product enters the store priced at these ten units. This assures aggregate balance between income in circulation and goods in stores.

But, we are also concerned with another kind of balance. Goods are not perfect substitutes for each other, and it would be pointless for the aggregate value of goods in stores to correspond to aggregate income in circulation, if consumers demanded goods that were in short supply–as they have a right to do–while stores had surpluses of other goods. The state would therefore have to produce not only an aggregate output corresponding to aggregate income in circulation, but also as much of each good as consumers demanded, given their incomes. This means that the state would have to look after balance of supply and demand of individual goods, even though aggregate balance was assured by the fact that a work unit would function as monetary unit (cost unit, price unit, income unit). It also means that the state would have to guide production and allocate resources in accordance with this fact, i.e., toward production of goods in greater demand, and away from those in smaller demand, so as to keep in balance consumption and production of individual goods.

In its capacity as producer, the state would thus perform the following functions:

1. Manage production economically, which means maximization of output and minimization of labor input.

2. Maintain balance between consumption and production of individual goods by appropriate guidance of production.

These are purely technical rather than economic tasks. The state would operate numerous plants but no *economic units.* Economic units make decisions with respect to satisfaction of different wants on the basis of their importance (value), relative to the principle of valuation–the economic objective. Private business enterprises decide which wants to satisfy on the basis of prospective returns, in pursuing their end of making profit. The solidarist state must decide, on the basis of objective utility, how far it wishes to carry production in exercising care for the nation's life, health, and culture (its economic objective). But the cooperative state makes no value judgments; it does not decide how far to go in producing different goods, because such decisions are made by subjective valuations of individual consumers. Consumers make decisions on the basis of subjective relative utility, in accordance with their objective of personal satisfaction. This is why we said that cooperative production depends on subjective decisions. The cooperative state is not an economizer but a technician; it acts mechanically to keep balance of consumption and production and solve the technical problem of an optimal relationship between the volume of output and the quantity of labor. For this reason the system is also known as *technocracy* (government by technicians).

The need to balance consumption and production of individual goods, and hence to allocate production and productive resources, implies that while each member of cooperative society may have the right to work, he does not have a right to a specific job that he would himself choose. He has a right to the work that has been assigned or will be assigned to him, and this applies also to changing jobs. The right to work exists, but freedom of choice of work does not. Labor is not obligatory, and in this negative sense it is free. I.e., if an individual does not want to work, he does not have to. He will of course starve unless someone can be found to work for him. However, there is no positive freedom of work; individuals are not free to choose their work. The cooperative state tries to match jobs and workers in accordance with workers' abilities. This follows from its objective of producing economically (maximum output with minimum labor input). But this involves different valuation than the solidarist assignment of work in accordance with relative disutility (to be considered below). In the cooperative system no individual is therefore forced to work, though he may be forced to do so de facto, and in that sense labor is free. Everyone has a right to work but not the right to choose his work. Freedom of choice of work is absent, and in that sense labor is not free.

As we saw, the balance of production and consumption in the cooperative system is not established by prices but by the state, administratively, using cooperative techniques. Aggregate balance is established simply because the money unit is not a quantity of some good or several goods (obtainable through exchange in a competitive market) but rather some quantity of work. The money unit is a unit of work. The only production costs are labor costs, and hence the number of work units used to produce a product is its price. In the cooperative system prices of goods are therefore determined by cost of production, i.e., labor cost. This is not so in capitalism where prices are equilibrium prices. Prices determine what costs can be incurred in producing goods, if producers are to be compensated, from sales, for the costs incurred. In the cooperative system goods have prices because production involves labor costs, and cooperative prices are equal to labor costs. In capitalism labor has a price because labor is required to produce goods that are sold at a price. Of course, cooperative valuation (pricing) is a technical problem.

While the capitalist money unit is based on goods, and the cooperative money unit on labor, individual consumers in both systems see money as some amount of purchasing power, expressed as a standard of living in miniature (a set of consumer goods in relation to money income). As far as the consumer is concerned, prices are "given"-even in capitalism—though he may have participated in their formation. But, his role in price formation is minor because he is only one among many. In national cooperation prices are given, as far as he is concerned, by a norm, namely the relationship of price and labor cost, over which he has no control. In both systems money is distinguished from other goods by its indirect abstract usefulness. "Indirect" refers to the fact that its utility does not derive from the physical tokens of which it is made (metal, paper, cooperative scrip) but is derived indirectly, from the goods that can be bought with the tokens. This usefulness is "abstract" because—in principle—any good can be purchased with money. Such conceptual characteristic applies also to cooperative money, but not to certificates in pure solidarism. Of course, the source of money's purchasing power is different in the two systems. In capitalism it derives from the fact that money is based on goods, whereas in the cooperative system it is based on labor.

For example, if the capitalist monetary unit is defined as some quantity of gold (the gold standard), then the valuation of gold is also technical, i.e., given by the relationship between the weight of gold valued and the weight of the (gold) monetary unit. E.g., if the monetary unit is defined as one gram of gold, the price of a kilogram of gold is 1000 units of money. Prices of goods other than gold are a function of the exchange ratio between gold and the goods. This is once again the outcome of subjective valuation.

On the other hand, the cooperative monetary unit is based on labor. It is defined as some amount of labor of a particular kind (labor, like goods, is heterogeneous) e.g., as one hour of unskilled labor. But how are other kinds of labor to be valued? In capitalism money is used to value not only different goods but also different kinds of labor and valuation of labor is based on the value of the goods that labor produces. In the last analysis, the value of labor—as it emerges in the labor market—is therefore also derived from subjective valuation. On the other hand, in the cooperative system goods are valued according to the quantity of labor embodied in them, and hence their valuation is technical. But what is the principle according to which are valued various kinds of labor? This is relevant for the valuation of goods whose production requires labor of different kinds, and it is therefore necessary to know the value relationships of one kind of labor to another for the purpose of determining the prices of such goods (e.g., the relationship of an hour of mental work to an hour of manual work, etc.). It is also necessary to possess such knowledge for the purpose of distribution of labor's compensation (incomes).

The system of national cooperation cannot provide an answer to this question. Although it originates in the claim that labor is, and ought to be, the only just basis for distribution of goods, it lacks a basis for the valuation of different kinds of labor. Indeed, the system does not even possess a fixed and stable work unit. The definition of the work unit as some length of time is quite indeterminate in view of variability of work performance.

The cooperative system is based on the ethical concept of deservingness of labor and for this reason must be included among individualistic systems. Solidarism, on the other hand, does not accept merit as the basis for distribution. It recognizes only objective, passive need. But what is "merit", and how is it measured? It can be expressed either as subjective disutility or as the objective result of labor. Subjective disutility (of two workers or two jobs) cannot be objectively expressed or measured, and is therefore of no help here. As for the results of labor, we speak of merit only if we attribute to such results (the products) positive value. (In case of negative value we speak of blame.) But then both merit and the value of labor are derived from the value of products, the results of labor, whereas we require the value of labor as the basis for the value of products. Furthermore, the system lacks any basis for objective valuation of the importance of goods which might be used to determine the merit of labor (to impute value to labor).

The technical nature of the cooperative guidance of production has led to the notion of defining the work unit in technical or physical terms (e.g., and "erg"), but this is clearly inappropriate when mental work is considered.

In capitalism the valuation of different kinds of labor is determined by equilibrium in the labor market, in accordance with demand and supply of labor. Higher wages induce workers to seek more training. There is also found unusually high compensation for special performance and rare talent (the case of unique labor) even without special subjective merit. But all this occurs within the framework of subjective valuation of goods from which derives the value of labor required for their production. None of this exists in the system of national cooperation.

It is easier to say that the cooperative system brings justice to labor, by simply attributing to labor the entire national product, than to discover a just principle of distribution among different workers. Once the conflict with capitalism ceases, there is danger that the workers' attention will turn inward, since the state is unable to bring about the differential valuation of labor, except arbitrarily, or perhaps by pursuing non-cooperative ends which are automatically achieved in capitalism through derivation of the value of labor from the value of goods. It will be necessary as well to pay high compensation for exceptional performance, and for "ideas which require no effort" but bring major benefits to the nation, to labor, and to the national product. But this involves the *economic* objective of care to maintain and improve the nation's life rather than a *technical* task.

Nor can the cooperative economy manage without capital (machines, engines, etc.). If regression is to be avoided, the cooperative economy must replace capital and if progress is to take place, capital must be expanded. But capital cannot be created differently than in capitalism—by labor and by saving. But in capitalism capital formation is financed from realized money incomes. Some part of these is shifted by their recipients from consumption to savings (invested at interest). The borrowers of capital funds take the consumer's place in the market and change resource allocation by using the borrowed funds in their enterprises (e.g., to build factories rather than residential housing). Enterprises may also engage in direct capital formation out of retained earnings.

In pure national cooperation, consumers would not be interested in saving and capital formation. The state itself would have to save and undertake capital formation directly, simply by not distributing to labor "the whole proceeds", or by charging prices higher than labor cost. This would be a heavy tax. Prior to World War II direct and indirect private capital formation in this country [Czechoslovakia] amounted to about one-half of the government budget. To match such levels, taxes would have to be raised accordingly. If the cooperative state tried to avoid this by borrowing from its citizens, it would be restoring private financial capital, and this would in turn diminish labor's return by the amount of interest paid.

When national cooperation involves centralized state control, it is at once a consumers' and a producers' cooperative, since the national collective participates in it both as producer and as consumer. However, the system may also be decentralized. In that case, it is "national" only in the sense that all business enterprises are replaced by workers' cooperatives. These could attempt to increase their incomes at the expense of consumers. The state would then be forced to assume the role of a regulatory (coordinating) agency, determining wages, prices, production and capital formation in the individual cooperatives, and the transfer of workers–otherwise competitive behavior would emerge. Without such coordinating agency the cooperatives would be essentially corporations with shares allocated to workers according to their labor and whose profits would show up as higher labor compensation.

In political practice, national cooperation, and the movement that urges its adoption, are traditionally described as communism. But this is incorrect. Were it correct, how would we describe solidarism? On the contrary, national cooperation and capitalism are individualistic systems which stand opposed to solidarism. Their foundation is self-responsibility. The individual is responsible for his own welfare. This is the opposite of solidarism where individuals, and the nation, are objects of care exercised by the state. National cooperation differs from capitalism in its system of production, in that production by business enterprise is replaced by cooperative production.

IV. THE SOLIDARIST SYSTEM

Let us first consider the solidarist critique of individualistic systems, particularly capitalism. It differs from the critique from which stems national cooperation. The starting point of the latter is the principle of justice and individual merit, that is, labor merit, and hence the demand of the right to the "undiminished proceeds of labor", hostility to non-labor incomes, demand of a universal right to work, etc. The point of departure is the postulate that each individual is responsible for his own destiny and should exercise care for his own welfare, but that labor represents the only just basis for distribution of income and the only genuine merit. The basic premise of national cooperation is therefore individualism.

The critique which is at the basis of solidarism is fundamentally different. Unlike individualism, it does not stand on the premise of personal merit and responsibility, the principle that everyone should be responsible for his own welfare. Were it based on that, it could not denounce as evil the co-existence of wealth and luxury on one hand, and poverty and deprivation on the other, regardless of why this was so, and what was the source of personal wealth. The solidarist point of departure is thus the postulate that there ought not to be luxury and wealth for some, when poverty and deprivation afflict others. But how could one blame the rich for being rich (when there are the poor and under-privileged) unless one's initial premise was that both the rich and the poor are part of a collective (community, nation) that should develop evenly toward the ideal of life, health and culture, and that departures from such even development—in either direction—are harmful?

Like solidarism the cooperative system also involves a relationship of mutuality among society's members. It is a relationship of mutual cooperation and aid, but does not involve the sacrifice of one individual for another or for the collective. One helps one fellow man in return for the same kind of help received from him, and both grow stronger through cooperation. The cooperative critique [of capitalism] does not denounce income inequality, if it is due to labor rather than property. It stands on the premise of labor merit. Solidarism, denounces all inequity (not necessarily inequality),* but does not at all propose the criterion of merit.

Every critique implies a value judgment based in each case on a particular objective. It indicates whether the particular economic system that is being evaluated corresponds to such objective, and if so, to what degree. The principle of valuation, the objective, from which the above critique is derived (that the coexistence of wealth and poverty is evil) can only be the ideal of life, health, and culture of the whole nation. From this objective, as ordering principle, follows solidarism and the nexus of personal solidarity among society's members. It leads to the ideal of balanced development of all members of the community, an ideal which is rather sensed when the critique is articulated and when it gains support.

The solidarist critique is directed against capitalism because there has not been as yet an opportunity to evaluate systems of national cooperation. However, its arguments are not directed against capitalism as such, but against individualism, and hence it also applies to the inequities in national cooperation. This is so because solidarism stands opposed to individualism, while national cooperation stands opposed to capitalism only within the framework of individualism.

Consistent solidarism means that all care for maintaining and improving the nation's life is exercised, for the whole nation, within a single state

---

* See p. 10.

economy. The nation is the object of care of such economy whose purpose is the ideal of life, health and culture. This purpose is the valuation principle wherein converge all particular sub-goals (needs) of such care, and which is the point of departure of all valuation in this economy. Its task is to allocate the nation's resources to the production of various goods, to assign work to members of the solidarist society, and to distribute to them the fruits of labor. Different needs are satisfied by producing different goods according to the principle of material solidarity, i.e., up to the point of equalization of *objective* relative marginal utilities. In other words, one must not pursue any further the satisfaction of a need, if relatively greater utility can be obtained by channeling production to another, and this implies equalization of relative marginal utilities.

Since the solidarist purpose is objective, all valuation in the solidarist economy, which is derived from this purpose, is also objective. Consequently, when we speak of utility, disutility, cost, return, etc., we mean *objective* utility, disutility, cost, etc., expressed by increments of life, health, and culture.

However, the utility problem is more complex here. What is at issue are not only different needs but also different individuals to whom various goods are allocated and who derive unequal utilities from consuming them. They do not have identical needs for goods. What we have in mind here are passive, objective needs. A person without a suit of warm clothes has a greater need of it than another who already possesses such a suit even though it is old. The former is found to be in need. Only if each had a suit of warm clothes would it make sense to think of a second suit. Here, too, one must not pursue the exercise of care for an individual, satisfying his passive needs more fully, if the consumption of another individual appears to yield more utility. While satisfying one need, e.g., food, the solidarist economy must, therefore also pay attention to other needs, e.g., housing. But, in addition to this, while satisfying the passive needs of an individual, it must also pay attention to satisfying the needs of others. In the former case, satisfaction of different needs converges in the nexus of material solidarity; in the latter, care for the different individuals converges in the nexus of personal solidarity, which imparts to the whole system the character and name of solidarism.

Curing a sick person represents objective utility for the state, for the state economy, whether or not the patient himself derives subjective utility from it, because it represents an increase in life and health, the objective pursued by the solidarist economy. Consequently, if an individual harms someone's health, he commits a criminal offense, even though the injured person may have consented to it. It is not the subjective interest of the injured person which is being protected (actually, if he consents he is not being subjectively injured), but the interest of the state. A "state value" is diminished. This applies even in the case of damage, such as theft, etc., of goods allocated by the state to a specific individual, because the state derives utility, given its objective, from the goods being enjoyed by that individual alone. The latter is not allowed to dispose of them nor to consent (ex post) to their being disposed of or damaged by a third party.*

When utility is defined in this way, then cost—which represents disutility, a decrease in the attainment of the objective which is associated with obtaining resources—is defined analogously. Consequently, in the solidarist economy, cost is defined as decrease in life, health and culture of the nation as a whole as well as of individuals. This point should be particularly noted, because it is very significant for understanding partial solidarism within the state economy, which is discussed below. Cost is associated with labor which produces all the resources of the solidarist economy. Labor cost is therefore the decrease of life, health and culture of the workers which results from their labor. Consider two workers. The one to whom a particular kind of work causes less disutility, harm to his health, etc., has a greater capacity to perform such work. Consequently, when we say that labor is assigned to members of the solidarist society according to their work capacity, we mean that it is assigned in accordance with relative objective cost, so as to minimize such cost (lower cost is preferred to higher cost). In the case of human beings, objective cost is an increasing function of the amount of work. Consequently,

---

* The problem in criminal law concerning consent to damage cannot be solved without considering the economic system in which the rule is to apply. As was shown, the solution in an individualistic system—where the interest of the individual is being protected—will be different from the solution in the solidarist system.

one cannot continue to assign more work to one worker if such work, assigned to another worker, would cause less disutility (cost). One cannot consider the work and the labor cost of one worker, without considering the potential work and labor cost of another. Members of the solidarist community are therefore in a nexus of personal solidarity, not only with respect to utility derived from consumption, but also with respect to the costs incurred in producing goods.

Each labor unit expended involves relative costs (decrease of life, health, etc.) that rise, starting from the lowest, and thus form a series of increasing relative costs. On the other hand, each unit of expended labor yields relative utility in the goods that it produces (increase of life, health and culture). Starting from the highest, these utilities form a decreasing series. Initially relative labor cost is low, while relative utility expressed in identical labor units is high. But subsequently, the difference diminishes until relative cost equals relative utility. The two series intersect at a point which represents the boundary of economic rationality. It is irrational to produce additional goods if their cost exceeds their utility. Hence, this boundary also represents the limit of resources available to the economy. This is also very important for understanding partial solidarism within the state sector, where the boundary of rationality appears as a tax-free minimum income, to be discussed below. It can be shown graphically:

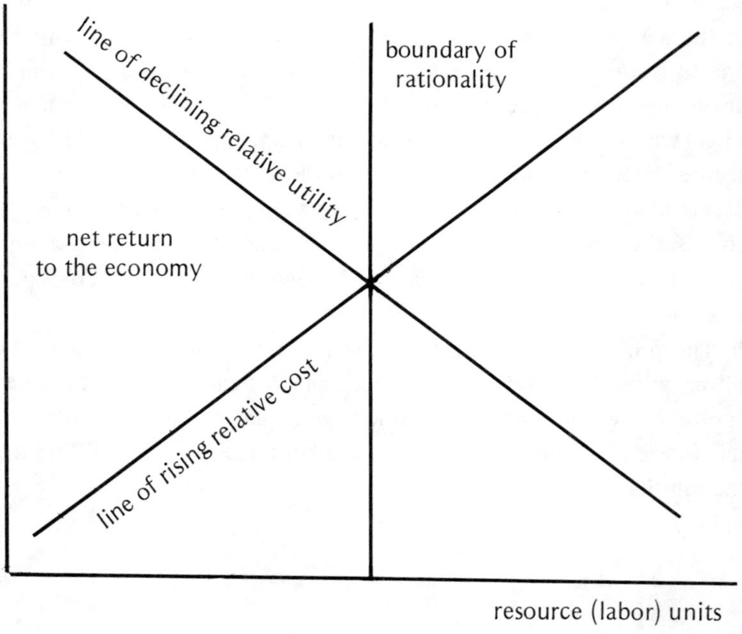

Beyond the boundary of rationality utility is below cost, and there is no net return [Translator's note: actually, net return is negative]. This end-oriented approach is applicable wherever activity is ruled by maximization of some end. It is actually a representation of the principle of economizing, and is therefore applicable to any economy though, of course, both utility and cost have different contents, depending on the ruling objective. In an economy whose purpose is subjective personal satisfaction, utility and cost have subjective contents (increase and decrease of satisfaction); in an economy whose objective is the making of money (private business enterprise) the end is objective (to make money), and so are the contents of utility and cost (increase and decrease of money). The purpose of the solidarist economy is also objective, though its content is not money but the ideal of the nation's life, health and culture. Consequently, solidarist utility and cost also have an objective content: Increase or decrease of life, health and culture. We are accustomed to think of costs as the costs of a business enterprise and hence to express all costs in money terms. As a result, we tend to think of solidarist costs as money costs, but that is incorrect. More will be said about this below.

The boundary of rationality represents the limit of satisfaction of different needs (both quantitatively and qualitatively) of individual members of the community and the solidarist state as a whole. Each member of the solidarist community is guaranteed his livelihood within this framework. He is endowed with the so-called *right to a living*, though it is inaccurate to speak of a "right" (i.e., subjective right) when the individual is the object of care. With respect to the volume and structure of its consumption content, the solidarist "right to a living" is a function of the collective's productive potential, as expressed by the boundary of rationality, and the valuation of the care-exercising agent. Consequently, the "living" need not be restricted to a level necessary to sustain bare life, if the collective's production potential permits a higher level. For the same reason, the converse of the right to a living–a tax-free minimum living standard–i.e., a level which ought not be reduced by taxation–will be different in different communities, districts, etc., depending on their productive potential.

The solidarist "right to a living", i.e., the consumer goods allocated to individual members of the solidarist society, is not a function of their productive contribution. The individual is sustained by the collective economy because of his need, not because he deserves such support by contributing his labor. Support based on merit would not represent distribution based on objective utility of the solidarist state and it would be a violation of its utility system. But this does not mean that individuals do not have an obligation to make productive contributions. Indeed, besides the bounty of nation, the only other source of all wealth is the labor of the community's members, and the solidarist economy must allocate labor so as to minimize labor cost (the disutility of labor). As we saw, this will be so when labor is allocated in accordance with relative costs, i.e., the capacity to work. (Each labor task is assigned to the individual who incurs thereby the least disutility.) Within this framework, each has an obligation to work, and the obligation to work according to his capacity is thus a corollary of the right to a living, in the sense in which minimum cost is a corollary of maximum utility. Solidarist consumption is not determined by merit, according to each individual's contribution to the national product, but according to objective (passive) need and the objective utility of the care-exercising agent. By the same token, work is not assigned in accordance with how much each member of society receives but solely in accordance with his objective capacity to work. This is necessary to minimize the economy's costs of securing resources (to minimize decreases of culture, health and life). The rationale of the obligation to work is thus not only the fact that only a rare individual would be willing to work when he was guaranteed a living, and must therefore have an obligation to work. The rationale must also include the capacity to work.

Under such circumstances, there can be no question that freedom to work does not exist. Since there are no sources of income other than labor, the individual is not only compelled to work de facto–as in the system of national cooperation–but he is also compelled *directly* by the solidarist society. His livelihood being guaranteed, he is not compelled to work through concern about it. Society compells him to work because labor is the only source of the joint subsistence fund. Hence, here too, there is physical assignment of work, and the individual is not free to choose his job. However, the principle of assigning work differs from that in national cooperation. It is not part of the cooperative purpose to assign work so as to cause to individuals the least decrease of life, health and culture (as in solidarism), but to maximize their performance. This implies a different kind of "carrying power". Were one to allocate a load equally among several differently endowed beasts of burden, one would not attain maximum utilization of "carrying power", because the "carrying power" of the strongest would be under-utilized, while the weak would carry excees burdens and collapse under them. Allocation according to individual "carrying power" increases the "carrying power" of the collective. By the same token, assigning work according to dexterity, skill, etc., but without paying attention to its disutility to the workers (which must be considered in solidarism), increases productivity of labor as a whole. In a purely cooperative economy, labor would be assigned to workers as loads are assigned to beasts of burden, by following the objective of economizing in production through minimization of labor costs. But the solidarist state would pay attention to the fact that individuals to whom the burden of labor is assigned are objects of its care directed to the ideal of life, health and culture. The cooperative state behaves the way it does because it is not concerned with the disutility of the workers. It pays no more attention to them than to beasts of burden. The solidarist state which is concerned, in using resources, only with the life, health and culture of the nation must consider the disutility of individuals resulting from work assigned to them.

Solidarist society is sometimes defined as a system in which each contributes according to his ability and receives according to his need. This definition is not incorrect, but without further specifying what is meant by "ability" and "need" it is too vague. "Ability" means capacity to work, as evaluated by the care-exercising agent, according to objective loss (of life, etc.) as the cost of labor assigned to the individual. "Need" means objective, passive need, as determined by the valuation of the care-exercising agent, according to his view of an individual's satisfaction, as yielding more or less objective utility.*

---

* When economics textbooks define need as "awareness of a want" and the drive to achieve its satisfaction, rather than desire to obtain the means to an end, and when these same textbooks define solidarism as a system in which each receives according to his need, the reader is bound to think of need as "subjective want." And yet it is clear that in a solidarist society goods cannot be distributed according to subjective want. Without a teleological conception of need (subjective need or objective need–depending on the systemic purpose) there is no way out of this confusion.

Consequently, members of the solidarist society, are not equal either with respect to consumption–which depends on their objective passive needs determined by objective utility of the care-exercising agent–or with respect to work assigned to them in accordance with their capacity. Nevertheless, solidarist society tends toward balanced development of its members directed toward the ideal of life, health and culture. A particular distribution of goods and assignment of work corresponds to such balanced development. Hence, from this standpoint, any other would be harmful. This is the solidarist meaning of the term "balanced" allocation.

All discretionary acts of the care-exercising agent vis-a-vis society's members as objects of its care, distribution of consumer goods and assignment of work, take place within a unitary economy, where there is no exchange (of goods for goods, goods for labor, goods and labor for money), and hence no money. Due to its complexity, such economy may make use of written orders and vouchers (for some amount of a good) but these are not money. Such vouchers could constitute an asset if they were required for consumption. They would be an *indirect* asset similar to railway tickets. But, they would not be an indirect *abstract* asset because they would not entitle their bearers to free choice of goods (as cooperative money still does).

In a technical sense, the solidarist economy can be partitioned into a sector of producing goods (solidarist production) and a sector of using goods (solidarist consumption). These two sectors are integrated in the solidarist economy as a whole. The consumption sector operates on the basis of relative objective utility, and the production sector operates on the basis of relative objective cost. The junction of the two sectors is formed by the boundary of rationality.

V. A COMPARATIVE SURVEY OF THE MOST IMPORTANT ELEMENTS OF ECONOMIC SYSTEMS

Control of goods is an aspect of the nation's economic order, of its economic system. Differences in the control of goods, of ownership, are so apparent in different economic systems that the systems have usually been described in terms of that control. In this connection, the point that was usually stressed was whether property was private (individual) or social (collective). Accordingly, individualism was usually opposed to collectivism. The system of national cooperation which we include, for excellent reasons, among individualistic systems, was usually classified, along with solidarism, as collectivist. Another distinction was usually drawn between the ownership of producer goods and that of consumer goods. When ownership of both was in the hands of the state (society) the literature spoke of *communism.* When the state owned only the means of production the literature spoke of *socialism* (K. Diehl). True, a distinct type of control of goods is found in each economic system, but systems cannot be described in terms of such control alone, since such control is only one of the characteristics of a particular system. Indeed, different systems (state capitalism, national cooperation, etc.) are compatible with one and the same form of control.

A contrast is drawn between individual (private) ownership and collective (common, public, state, etc.) ownership. We shall refer to state ownership, the state being the agent who either exercises total care for maintenance and improvement of the nation's life (solidarism), or merely provides the means to serve the ends of individual households (national cooperation).*

In individualistic capitalism, all control of goods is in private hands. Goods are owned privately, either by households or business enterprises. Enterprise assets (even when productively employed outside the enterprise–e.g., deposits) are capital. Even the state–when it acts as private individual–*is* a "private individual".

In national cooperation, there are no business enterprises, and the production of consumer goods takes place in state establishments. Prior to their transfer–through purchase–to the household sector their control must be in the hands of the state. Households can only purchase consumer goods, which implies that private ownership is conceptually restricted to these goods. Goods used to produce other goods (which are owned by private business enterprises in capitalism) are excluded from commerce and hence cannot be privately owned (e.g., machinery). But the boundary line is fluid, since households also engage in various productive activities (sewing machines, meat grinders). Hence, the cooperative system cannot be described in terms of individual or collective ownership of particular categories of goods. It can only be described in terms of the system of the production of goods. Goods are produced by state establishments rather than private business enterprises.

There is no capital–in the sense of assets owned by private enterprises–in the cooperative system. There are no private enterprises, and assets used in state establishments are not employed to make money (which is different from state capitalism). Hence, the capital of former private businesses not only is state-owned, but ceases to be capital (in the capitalist sense). Alternatively, we could refer to the assets of state establishments as "capital", but it would be "capital" with a very different meaning.

National cooperation does not exclude individual financial capital (in the capitalist sense), that originates in the savings and credit

---

* We also refer to state capitalism, but this is not a distinct economic system.

relationships of consumers. Indeed, there is a question of how the state would obtain resources for new investment and new equipment required to raise productive capacity beyond existing equilibrium levels, i.e., for technical progress. A portion of resources would not be used for current consumption but for investment. Labor would have to give up its claim to such output, notwithstanding its "right to undiminished proceeds." The state could compel labor to part with this portion of output which implies cooperative taxation: either direct or indirect taxes leading to higher prices of consumer goods. Alternatively the state could borrow the required funds. In the latter case, there would be both financial capital and interest and hence, national cooperation would not abolish non-labor incomes. It would only abolish business profit. This is the case in Russia today where the state borrows from the citizens.

In a purely solidarist system, the state must have control of all goods, both in their production and consumption, because production and consumption occur within a unitary state economy. The state allows individual members of solidarist society to enjoy goods, but they are not allowed to do so at their discretion, to use them or not to use them as they see fit, to convey them to others, etc. (This they can do in the system of national cooperation). The situation is analogous to that of a father who provides clothes for his child and may take them away at any time (e.g., to give them to a younger child). In solidarism consumption is a citizen's duty as well as his right, a right protected against all who would infringe upon it. But, as we shall see, this does not imply private ownership. Individuals only have a right to a particular good in the sense that they are permitted to enjoy it, such right being simultaneously a duty: A duty vis-a-vis the state, a right vis-a-vis other citizens (protection against infringement).

The solidarist state would obtain investment resources required for economic progress from the labor of its citizens over which it has direct control. It would restrict current consumption to obtain from currently expended labor the resources needed to raise productivity and future consumption. It could not raise investment funds by borrowing from the citizens, since they have no funds (there is no money).

There are thus various shades of control of goods which cannot be expressed in terms of concepts of civil law, such as private ownership, the right to use someone else's property, etc. Private ownership as such (in the meaning of civil law) exists only in capitalism (for all goods) and in national cooperation (for consumer goods). This form of ownership implies that an agent may use goods as he sees fit. Conceptually–if there is no specific prohibition–he may destroy them, convey them to others, enjoy them, etc. His interests are protected (he is protected in his use of goods) against theft, robbery, and damage. But, when these occur with his consent, no criminal offense has taken place. Goods distributed to citizens of the solidarist state do not represent such ownership, even though the citizens may be given the right to make full use of them. But they *must* use them. They must neither destroy them nor transfer them to others. When a third party damages goods he commits a criminal offense, even when he does so with the consent of the citizen entitled to their use. This form of "ownership" has a very different meaning.

State (collective) control of goods–whether in solidarism or in national cooperation–is not the same kind of ownership as that which private individuals enjoy in capitalism. State ownership does not serve here some "subjective" state purpose (no such purpose exists), and hence the state may not use the goods that it controls as it sees fit (e.g., it may not destroy them at will). The state is constrained by systemic norms prescribing how goods are to be used. Such norms are different in the cooperative system and in solidarism, but in either case there are certain duties which prevent unrestricted use of goods (a right with which private owners are conceptually endowed both in the capitalist and cooperative individualism).

2. The Position of Labor

We are concerned with two questions:

(a) the question of freedom to work versus obligation to work, of free choice of work versus compulsory assignment to a particular job; and,

(b) the question of the valuation of labor and its compensation in different economic systems.

Ad (a) *The question of freedom versus compulsion, free choice versus its absence, the right to work.*

With respect to this question, we must distinguish:

(a) Whether the worker can choose to work or not to work or whether he is compelled to work by the state (society). The former is the case of (1) freedom to work; the latter of (2) obligation to work.

(b) Whether the worker is free to choose his job or not; in the former case there is (1) free choice of job; in the latter (2) its absence. There are therefore four conceptual combinations:

I. a-1 freedom to work combined with b-1 free choice of job
II. a-1 freedom to work combined with b-2 absence of free choice of job
III. a-2 obligation to work combined with b-1 free choice of job
IV. a-2 obligation to work combined with b-2 absence of free choice of job

Case I corresponds to individualistic capitalism, Case II to national cooperation, and Case IV to solidarism. Case III is not possible for practical reasons (that an individual should be compelled to work but free to choose his job). In more ancient economic systems, with which our analysis is not concerned, there was also slavery, serfdom, corvée, etc.

By "freedom to work" we mean *legal* freedom. It is sometimes argued that workers in capitalism are not endowed with freedom to work because they own no property, and are therefore compelled to work by circumstances. They have no other way to make a living. This would also be true of national cooperation, where it would hold for everyone, since labor would be the only source of income. However, we mean by "freedom to work" the absence of legal compulsion, which is true both of capitalism and the cooperative system.

Freedom to work does not exist in solidarism. On the contrary, here there is obligation to work, a corollary of distribution of goods according to objective need. The solidarist obligation to work is also more exactly delimited, in the sense that everyone must work according to his capacity. The obligation to work at a particular job is imposed on those whose life, health and culture it injures less.

Thus delimited, the obligation to work includes, simultaneously, the absence of free choice of job. Workers are not endowed with this freedom. The decision to assign a citizen to a job is made by the decision maker of the solidarist economy on the basis of the principle that the job should cause him less disutility than it would to others, that he should work at a job for which he has greater capacity than others. Here the obligation to work and the absence of free choice of job derive from the same principle, the principle of capacity to work (minimization of disutility).

Free choice *of job* is also absent in national cooperation. But here it is combined with freedom *to work,* and hence there must be a special systemic principle of assigning jobs to individual workers. This principle is derived from the purpose of the national cooperative system, which consists of (1) achievement of partial equilibria of production and consumption of different goods, and corresponding guidance of production and of productive resources away from goods in excess supply to goods in short supply; and, (2) striving for productive efficiency (minimizing resource use). However, the equilibrium principle does not determine what job is to be assigned to each worker (from the viewpoint of equilibrium it is immaterial to which job a worker is assigned). It is productive efficiency which is relevant here. In agreement with the principle of productive efficiency and increasing productivity, work is to be assigned according to *ability,* which is not the same thing as *capacity* to work in the solidarist sense. The solidarist principle of assigning work according to capacity states that a specific job is to be assigned to the worker whose health and life it injures least. The cooperative principle of economizing labor states that a specific job is to be assigned to the worker who works faster, better, etc., regardless of how it affects his health.

It should be noted, in this connection, that in capitalism no individual is guaranteed that he will find a job because the demand for labor depends on the changing incentives of business enterprises to step up or cut down production, whereas the pool of job seekers is not so elastic. Hence unemployment exists, and the right to work does not. In national cooperation, the right to work is an obligation of the state, and hence there is no unemployment. In solidarism, where all are compelled to work, there is no point of speaking of the right to work as an obligation of the state, and there is of course no unemployment. There would also be no basis for losing the material base of one's livelihood due to loss of work, since all are guaranteed a living in accordance with the collective's productive capacity, as determined by the boundary of rationality. The right to a living is not merely a variation of the right to work. The right to work is an aspect of national cooperation, while the right to a living is an aspect of solidarism.

Ad (b) *The question how labor is valued and how it is compensated for work.*

Social valuation of labor in capitalism is reflected in the wage rate, the price of labor formed in the labor market, i.e., the exchange value of labor, derived from valuation by enterprises which buy labor. The exchange value of labor, the wage rate, is expressed in money terms, and it settles at an equilibrium point, the point where labor demanded and supplied at such wage rate are in balance. (We do not discuss here the question of different wage rates paid for different kinds of labor.) The chief buyers of labor are business enterprises which require labor to produce goods. They recover their costs from the value of their sales. After deducting the costs of material inputs used up in production (e.g., raw materials, auxiliary materials, depreciation of capital assets), what is left is the objective (net) return of the enterprise as a working team. From this comes the compensation of capital (determined in the money market) and the compensation of labor (determined in the labor market). The residual represents the personal return of the entrepreneur (to be distinguished from enterprise profit, because the personal return of the entrepreneur includes also compensation of his labor and capital). It follows that what enterprises are willing to pay for labor depends primarily on the price of the output that labor produces, because the price forms the overall framework of distribution by the enterprise. The value of labor derives from the value of the output that labor produces, not vice versa. Goods do not derive their value from the quantity of labor required for their production, and relative prices of different goods are not determined by relative quantities of labor "embodied" in them. On the contrary, labor is used and valued because it yields a valuable product.

This is connected with the question of the right to the "undiminished proceeds of labor". If, as Marx taught, prices of goods are determined by the quantity of labor embodied in them, i.e., by the value of such labor, then the entire price (the objective return of the enterprise) should go to labor. If entrepreneurs and capitalists also receive income this is at the expense of the return of labor, which does not get its full share. Labor is shortchanged and exploited. From this argument stems the demand for the "undiminished proceeds of labor". If the product does not derive its value from the value of labor (but the converse holds), then the price of the product is not simply the result of labor.

What is meant by the "return of labor"? When man faces nature as a free good, he views his entire product (harvest, catch), as the return to his labor, and credits this return to his labor alone. When a farmer observes that his neighbor, who works as hard as he does, but on less fertile ground, obtains a harvest only half the size of his, he will agree that half of his harvest is due to the superiority of his land. And, since superior land is not freely available, its owner will demand compensation from others who would use it. As a result, the return to labor [on the superior land] drops by one half. It follows, that the return to labor changes, depending on the viewpoint. A worker's return for his labor in an enterprise is his wage. From what viewpoint does the total product constitute the return of labor? This is the case from the viewpoint of the whole working nation. In that case, the relationships among individuals (such as shares of national wealth, shares of national income, various claims, etc.) disappear. The working nation as a whole "owns" all land and all means of production. Additional goods, produced on its land and with its means of production, are obtained only by its labor. We speak therefore of the return to the nation's labor, by which we mean the aggregate national product (of course, after deduction of inputs used up in the process of production). It is, somewhat, as if we viewed the whole nation as a single enterprise whose objective return (the objective return of the enterprise as a working team) we have in mind.

If the entire product is also to be regarded as the return of labor alone, in a single enterprise, then there cannot be individuals owning land and capital, facing those owning only their labor. Hence the demand that land and the means of production should cease to be privately owned, (which implies national cooperation) follows necessarily from the "right to the undiminished proceeds of labor". In the cooperative system, as we know, the exchange value of goods is derived from labor, and in principle there are no incomes other than labor incomes. Hence, the "right to the undiminished proceeds" of labor is realized.

In solidarism labor is valued as a means to achieve the purpose of the solidarist economy, as creating utility (a portion of the nation's life, health and culture). It is not valued in order to set its compensation, but because it yields a valuable product (which has an objective solidarist value), because it involves a cost (an expenditure of life and health), and because it must be used economically. In solidarism there is no connection between labor and its compensation. Indeed, there is no compensation of labor as such. When the worker receives a portion of the total product, this is not because he has worked to produce it, because he contributed to it, but because the state acknowledges his needs.

3. Economic Value

(a) Capitalism

Economics views value as if individualistic capitalism were the only economic system, and even then it fails to get to the bottom of the problem. But, each economic system has its own system of valuation.

In individualistic capitalism, valuation is most obvious when expressed by prices in a broad sense, e.g., prices of goods, prices of labor (wages), etc. The price of a good or the price of labor is its exchange value expressed in money. When we say that the price of a book is 100 crowns* we express its value in money. When we say this, we imply that some quantity of other goods, which can be purchased with that sum of money, can be exchanged for the good in question (prices being given). We see then that a good, or labor, possesses not only *direct* usefulness, a function of its physical characteristics (e.g., the usefulness of a ring used as an ornament), but also *indirect* usefulness, i.e., the usefulness of other goods obtainable in exchange for it (that can be purchased for the price of the good in question). The ring represents the food that could be obtained in exchange for it (for instance, during the war, urbanites saw a sweater as a potential goose). When exchange is universal, a good possesses either indirect *concrete* usefulness (e.g., a theatre ticket) or indirect *abstract* usefulness. The monetary unit is a measure of indirect abstract usefulness. The exchange value of goods (including labor), their indirect abstract usefulness, is expressed in money terms. Exchange value is the degree of indirect abstract usefulness which has its origin—under conditions of universal exchange—in the market mechanism and is expressed in terms of the monetary unit.

However, exchange value is not the only economic value in capitalism; it is not even the primary economic value. It is a reflection of exchange

---

* Translator's note: the "crown" is the name of Czechoslovakia's monetary unit.

mechanism which emerges and is sustained through the order of economic units that constitute the market environment and that are instrumental in the formation of prices. This order is the outcome of primary economic valuation, i.e., valuation by these economic units.

The market environment consists of, and prices are formed by, consuming economic units (households) and money-making economic units (enterprises). The order which rules these units is a function of the objective which they strive to attain. Households strive for the subjective end of personal satisfaction which molds wants, utilities, costs, value. The order that rules them is the outcome of subjective valuation, in accordance with the objective of personal satisfaction.

The second type of economic unit that constitute the capitalist market environment are money-making business enterprises. They strive to attain the objective end of making money. This end is central for the valuation of labor and goods within enterprises and it determines the ordering of all enterprise activities according to relative objective utilities and costs, i.e., increases and decreases of money. In this case, valuation and value are objective, in agreement with the objective nature of the purpose which is the starting point of valuation.

We do not consider here the fact that the state is also a buyer in the market, because in that case the state's economy represents partial solidarism. This would be a case of a mixed solidarist and capitalist system, whereas we are concerned here only with pure capitalism.

(b) National Cooperation

Properly speaking, household is the sole economic unit of the cooperative economy. It differs in no way from the capitalist household, and its behavior is ruled by subjective valuation. Workers, too, value the labor they perform for the state subjectively. On the one hand they consider a unit of their labor from the viewpoint of subjective utility which they expect to derive from the goods that can be purchased with the income received for their labor. On the other hand, they consider it from the viewpoint of their subjective cost (disutility). The decreasing series of utilities and the increasing series of costs determine jointly the subjective boundary of rationality of both work and consumption.

Here too there is an exchange mechanism, instituted by the state, for trading labor for goods from state stores on the basis of free choice.

Here too exchange is carried on with the aid of money which possesses exchange value (purchasing power). Each good, including labor, is valued in money terms. But, all these exchange relationships and the entire (limited) exchange mechanism do not emerge from the interactions of economic units in the market or from the order by which they are ruled, or from economic valuations that follow from their objectives. (In capitalism exchange value represents economic value, though a secondary one.) Here valuation of labor and goods in money terms is technical because the labor unit serves as monetary unit. A given quantity of labor is measured by this unit, and the value of a particular good is determined by the measured labor cost (expressed in the same units).

(c) Solidarism

In pure solidarism, there is only one economic unit—the state economy. Hence there is only one kind of economic value, attributed to labor and to goods by the economy's care-exercising decision maker in accordance with its objective. The economy's purpose (the ideal of the nation's life, health and culture) is objective, i.e., its content can be communicated. Hence, all economic concepts associated with this purpose are objective as well. Needs, utilities, costs, as well as value (the degree of utility or cost) are objective. Anyone can make critical judgments concerning the economy's purpose, and may offer to the state suggestions and advice in the field of applied economics, about the best way of attaining it.

The individual in the solidarist economy may also engage in subjective valuation of his (compulsory) labor and his rations of goods (which he must use). This may cause him psychic revulsion toward such compulsory labor and consumption. But he acts under compulsion and his behavior is not determined by such value considerations. Our concern is with the behavior of the solidarist state, why it decides on this or that course of action, and we are therefore concerned only with the state's economic valuation. In pure solidarism, there is no exchange value because there is no exchange.

4. Money in Different Economic Systems

Money is a medium of exchange, and it is therefore found only in economic systems where exchange exists. Where there is no exchange there is no money, though there may exist tokens which resemble money, e.g., paper vouchers, etc. There is no exchange in pure solidarism, and hence no money. Though individuals work for the solidarist state and receive goods in accordance with the state's conception of their needs, this does not constitute an exchange relationship. The latter assumes voluntariness and a relationship of material utility between what is given and what is received. This is not so in solidarism where there is no connection between what individuals give (their labor) and what they receive (according to their needs). They receive goods not because they have contributed anything but, irrespective of that, simply because they are considered to be in need. For the purpose of distributing goods, the solidarist economy may institute vouchers for particular goods, according to administrative requirements of the distribution process and the division of labor within it (e.g., one person may determine what the needs are, another may be employed in distributing the goods in the stores). However, such vouchers are not money, nor are they an analogue of money. Their external similarity to paper money is irrelevant. What is relevant is the intrinsic essence of the matter.

Exchange in the proper sense exists only in individualistic systems, capitalism and national cooperation. In capitalism it takes place between separate economic units; in the cooperative system individual households trade labor for goods provided by the state. In both cases, there is voluntariness (labor is not compulsory in the cooperative system) and there are utility relationships (in the cooperative system workers calculate whether the utility of goods they can get for their labor outweighs its disutility). Money facilitates exchange in both cases. Nevertheless, there is a fundamental and major difference between money in capitalism and money in national cooperation.

Capitalist money facilitates primarily the exchange of goods, whereas money in national cooperation facilitates only the exchange of labor for goods produced by labor, since no other exchange exists. This determines the nature of money. Capitalist money is, first of all, one of the goods. It is some quantity of a good with characteristics that make it most suitable for the function of facilitating exchange. It should be divisible, it should retain its physical characteristics over time, it should be commonly available and it should have a history of relatively stable exchange relationship with other goods. These are the characteristics of precious metals, particularly gold.

Eventually there evolves, with the aid of metallic money, an entire complex of economic magnitudes (prices, incomes, returns, etc). As a result, in making their daily purchases, people no longer even think about the metal content of currency, but only its purchasing power, i.e., the amount of consumer goods that it will buy. Consequently, metallic money may be not only supplemented but completely replaced by paper money, i.e., money made of a substance without any value, or by credit money, which no longer assumes a physical form, but is merely a unit of account used to transfer balances from one account to another. A unit of money then no longer represents some quantity of metal, but rather a certain purchasing power, a set of goods and services that it will buy. In addition to consumer goods, it can also buy labor, raw materials, and semi-fabricates. However, if we wish to compare the purchasing power of money and its changes over time, we must exclude from such comparison all intermediate items and, as it turns out, we can consider only final goods, i.e., goods in the stage in which they are purchased by households. Labor, too, is an intermediate item, and a unit of money represents a certain minimum living standard (the set of goods which makes up such standard).

In capitalism, labor cannot be the basis of money either in the sense of a labor unit being the monetary unit, or in the sense of the purchasing power of money being an expression of some quantity of labor. Speaking figuratively, one could say that paper currency is based "on labor"* because labor produces the national product. The latter, after deducting intermediate items, and dividing by an "economic magnitude" (national income in money terms), yields as quotient the money unit as an average miniature living standard.** The relationship of national product to

---

* During the inaugural meeting of our National Bank I said, addressing its governor, Dr. Pospíšil, that I was conveying to his care "the rarest jewel, the Czechoslovak crown, which is based neither on silver nor gold, but on labor." (In 1926 we had a nominalist paper currency.)

** Translator's note: The concept of *economic magnitude* is explained by the author in an earlier study, *Národní hospodářství [Economics]* (1st ed. 1940, 2nd ed. 1946) as follows:

national income is the only basis of the monetary unit once it has ceased to be an expression of some amount of gold (paper currency). The capitalist monetary unit cannot be based on labor in the way it is based on gold and on goods, because here labor derives its value from the value of goods, not vice versa.

> The fact that the modern capitalist economy uses money has led to the fact that we associate with each good the magnitude of its price, with each enterprise the magnitude of its return, with each household the magnitude of its income . . . there are three main series (levels) of these magnitudes, the series (level) of prices . . . the series of returns . . . and the series of incomes . . . the sum of all money incomes is equal to the sum of all prices (excluding intermediate items). We shall refer to each of the above, identical sums as *economic magnitudes.* These are the basic series of economic magnitudes (returns, prices, incomes); in addition to these there are other economic magnitudes (wages, etc.). . .pp. 73-75.

The concept of an *average miniature living standard* is explained as follows:

> The individual regards money from the viewpoint of the usefulness of the goods that he would purchase, in accordance with relative utilities . . . We cannot observe this internal notion of the individual other than ex post, by observing his actual expenditure of money, his consumption, his living standard, contrasted with the amount of money devoted to his consumption. A unit of money then represents a fraction of this consumption expenditure; it represents a certain *miniature living standard,* which differs from individual to individual, depending on their wants and on the amount of money they have available to spend . . . In addition to the individual, economic science and the policy maker also formulate conceptions of the value of the unit of money, particularly when they consider the changes that have taken place in this value . . . For economic science and the policy maker the unit of money represents also a certain *miniature living standard,* but—as distinct from the individual consumer—it is *an average living standard* determined by production and/or consumption of the aggregate of all consumer goods reduced by an economic magnitude (i.e., aggregate Consumption divided by nominal National Income). (pp. 78-80)

In national cooperation, where the value of goods is derived from the value of labor, the monetary unit is naturally a unit of labor. Some quantity of labor is the monetary unit in the same sense that some quantity of goods is the monetary unit in capitalism. Here the relationship between a unit of labor and prices of goods is not based on economic valuation (on exchange relations between different goods, and between labor and goods), but solely on technical valuation, i.e., calculation of the number of labor units used in producing a particular good. Hence, this relationship changes only when there is a change in the technique of production.

Workers are aware, not only of the technical basis of the monetary unit, i.e., some amount of gold in capitalism, or labor in national cooperation but, above all, its purchasing power (exchange value), i.e., the set of goods that a money unit will buy. These sets (the quantity of each good) are different for different individuals. Two individuals or two families with identical incomes do not buy identical sets, to "see" the monetary unit, i.e., the ratio of consumption to income, C/Y, as their consumption in miniature. They make expenditures in accordance with subjective valuation, purchasing sets of different compositions (different amounts of different goods). Changes in the structure of the purchasing power of money (how much of various goods money will buy) could result from changes in subjective valuation, as just noted, or from changes in production technique (increases or decreases of labor input required to produce various goods) leading to rising or falling prices.

Here too changes in purchasing power over time (with prices determined by the technical relationship of output and labor input) would be concerned only with prices of consumer goods bought by households. (For details about money, see the first volume of my *Soustava narodniho hospodarstvi [System of National Economy]* published in 1938.)

5. A Synoptic Survey

The synoptic survey outlines the order of the various economic systems in terms of conceptual elements which are then concurrently traced through the separate systems. The survey presents in concentrated form what was discussed above in extenso. It is particularly important to note the point which was already made, that capitalism and national cooperation belong to the individualistic order characterized by individual responsibility for one's welfare, and hence stand opposed to the solidarist order (communism).

We must not be misled by the fact that the cooperative system, which is opposed to capitalism *within* the framework of individualism, represents one of the aims of movements known as socialist. Socialism is not a distinct economic system which could be defined positively. It is simply opposition to capitalism, and includes any noncapitalist system, including national cooperation. The latter must be classified by economic science as belonging within the individualistic order, in view of its characteristic institution (individual responsibility for one's welfare).*

Consequently, socialist ideologies do not represent a single order, but two quite distinct orders, which have only one common feature: their opposition to capitalism. Hence they represent only a negation of capitalism, emphasizing only the formal circumstance that capitalism does not arise on the basis of a central plan, but spontaneously on the foundation of the price mechanism (using the term "price" in a broad sense), whereas all other systems classified as socialism (including national cooperation and solidarism) are based on central planning. This is why "planning", as a characteristic of socialism, is contrasted with capitalism. But, planning refers only to *form,* whereas *what* one plans is the *substance.* Consequently, "planning" cannot impart a unique meaning to socialism, if socialism includes two so thoroughly opposed systems: national cooperation and solidarism. One cannot "plan" unless one has chosen one or the other order to be "planned" for. It is the order which takes national precedence; it represents the content of the plan that is to be worked out. It is therefore, not legitimate to contrast "planning" with the capitalist order. Instead, capitalism must be contrasted with some other order for which the planning is done.

In practice, there are political parties that call themselves "socialist", whose political platform is democracy and which favor the business enterprise system in the economic sphere. But they are radically reformist in matters of social welfare policy. However, social-welfare policy presumes the existence of an individualistic system within whose framework it realizes some aspects of solidarism.

---

* I failed to do this myself (prior to the publication in 1938, of my *Soustava národního hospodářství [System of National Economy].*). Prior to that, I described only capitalism as an individualistic system.

VI. MIXED ECONOMIC SYSTEMS

Individualistic capitalism is primordial in the sense that, at all times and in all places, when civilization is destroyed and economic life starts afresh, capitalist institutions such as exchange, money, prices, business enterprises, consuming units, wages, etc., develop spontaneously. When no one else exercises care for the individual, he must exercise it himself. Similarly, when an alternative system, for example, national cooperation, is introduced, and it does not embrace all of economic activity (whether this is intentional or due to oversight), the resulting vacuum is immediately filled by capitalism, though perhaps capitalism of a rather primitive kind (e.g., the so-called "bazaars" in Russia). Individualistic capitalism generates very complex and intricate institutions, which have not, as yet, been fully understood by economic science. Nevertheless, it is not a system designed with a purpose in mind on the basis of a specific plan. It arises spontaneously from the interests and out of the order of economic units that constitute the market environment. All other systems are devised, purposive, planned. They have certain purposes which are to be achieved through them. They involve all of society (nation), and hence the problems faced by these systems are much more complex. Every disturbance of the social whole affects each system more than it affects capitalism, where disturbances are overcome, more or less, automatically.

conceptual elements	INDIVIDUALISM		SOLIDARISM (Communism)
agent and object of care for the individual and the nation	everyone (the individual) is an agent exercising care for himself (responsibility) for one's own welfare) according to subjective satisfaction as the purpose of such care		the nation is the object of care exercised by the state and directed towards the ideal of life, health and culture as the purpose of such care; (social responsibility for the individual)
	CAPITALISM	NATIONAL COOPERATION (ethnocracy, technocracy, etc.)	
organization of the system in which the care takes place	a) individual consuming units (households) use their income to purchase goods in the market systemic purpose: subjective satisfaction b) money-making economic units, enterprises, which produce all goods and generate all incomes systemic purpose: to make money	a) individual consuming units (households) use their income to purchase goods in state stores systemic purpose: subjective satisfaction b) state establishments where goods are produced and incomes generated technical systemic purpose: to maintain balance of production and consumption; to economize labor	a single state economy for the nation as a whole goods produced and consumed within this economy systemic purpose: the ideal of life, health, and culture of the nation
control of goods	all goods are privately owned, fully controlled by individual consuming units (consumer goods) or by money-making enterprises (capital goods)	goods used in production by state establishments owned by the state; goods bought by households for their purposes owned by households	all goods owned by the state
the order which results from valuation	a) consuming economic units have ends, goods, wants, utilities, returns, costs, (increases or decreases of satisfaction) of all which are subjective; the same is true of the degree of utility: value	a) the end and the valuation of consuming economic units is subjective, as in capitalism b) state establishments make technical valuations (measurements) in terms	there is objective economic value because the ideal of life, health, and culture is an objective economic ideal this holds analogously for utility

	b) money-making enterprises have an end (to increase the amount of money made) which is objective; this applies also to their requirements, utilities, value	of labor units c) goods valued according to labor input	(increase of life, etc.) for cost (decrease of life, etc.) for needs, etc.
exchange, money	exchange between all economic units money based on goods equilibrium prices	exchange only with the state: goods for labor money based on labor prices determined by labor cost	no exchange no money no prices
income	beside labor income there is entrepreneurial income and income from capital national product distributed according to the purchasing power of individuals derived from their labor, capital, and entrepreneurship; this is determined in the market	there is only labor income national product distributed solely on the basis of labor merit	no personal income goods allocated to individuals according to objective needs (seen from the viewpoint of the purpose of care for the nation's welfare)
labor; compensation, freedom, obligation, free choice, no free choice, "right to work" "right to the undiminished proceeds of labor"	labor is free and there is free choice of job the "right to work" does not exist the "right to the undiminished proceeds of labor" does not exist	labor is free, but there is no free choice of jobs (workers are assigned jobs according to their ability) the "right to work" is put into effect (there is no other income but labor income the "right to the undiminished proceeds of labor" is put into effect (the total product goes to labor)	work is compulsory and there is no free choice of job (workers assigned jobs according to their capacity to work) the "right to work" is superfluous "the right to the undiminished proceeds of labor" does not exist; there is no connection between labor performed and its compensation (rations of goods)
the right to a living	the right to a living does not exist	the right to a living does not exist	the right to a living is put into effect
	CAPITALISM		SOCIALISM

Non-capitalist systems require a higher degree of organization if the entire economy is to be effectively controlled by the nation. This is easier when the technical level of production is higher, and when production is concentrated in large-scale enterprises, rather than dispersed in primitive small-scale ones. For this reason anti-capitalist pressures concentrate primarily on large-scale enterprises.

The nation's care to maintain and improve its life does not have to be organized in a single distinct system. Systems can be mixed; one may be applied in one sector, a different one in another sector. Indeed, such mixed economies are, historically, the rule. Consistent and pure economic systems, such as those described above, are found nowhere.

In some countries, individualistic capitalism continues to be supplemented by partial cooperation through cooperatives and public corporations, and by solidarism (the fiscal system, social-welfare policy, direct controls, etc). Elsewhere the system may be based on national cooperation and state capitalism, supplemented by private capitalism (private craftsmen employing no labor, borrowing by the state from its citizens), as well as solidarism. The literature of social reform contains a number of proposals which imply mixed economies. Agrarian socialists (Henry George and others) wanted to expropriate only land, Charles Hall proposed a ban on the production of luxuries, Popper-linkeus wanted everyone to be subject to compulsory labor service for a few years, etc.

One way to counter criticism of capitalism is to supplement it with solidarism, thus removing its worst shortcomings. Social welfare policy represents implementation of solidarist elements on a capitalist foundation. Combination of systems is thus a fact of daily life, and it appears that development proceeds between the two poles of individualism and solidarism, between the individual's and the nation's will to live, since one depends on the other.

The question arises whether systems can be combined at will or whether there exist limits of the mixed economy. Every economic system is made up of a number of congruous links, and it is clear that one cannot combine randomly an element of one system with an element of another, in the belief that one can thus create a new, or a mixed system. One cannot put into effect the right to the undiminished proceeds of labor and retain, at the same time, the business enterprise system. One cannot distribute goods in accordance with labor performed and allocate them, at the same time, according to subjective need. One cannot enact a universal right to a living in capitalism, because many people, perhaps the majority, would prefer living without working rather that working for a wage, and it would become necessary to introduce a compulsory labor. The grafting of an alien element onto a particular economic system leads to its disintegration and transformation into one for which the grafted element is appropriate. Enactment of the "right to work" in capitalism would lead to breakdown of the capitalist system, and transfer of production to state establishments. E.g., during the February 1884 revolution in France, the right to work was hastily enacted; it had to be withdrawn as early as June 21, while heavy fighting went on in the streets of Paris (Dr. Anton Menger: *Das Recht auf den vollen Arbeitsertrag,* 1904, p. 23).

Such alien element tending to subvert the business enterprise system, is also the organization by employees of enterprise workers' councils, which engage not only in the defense of workers' interests, but also take over the entrepreneurial function (totally or in large part). For practical purposes, the enterprise is thus transformed (without expropriation) into a producers' cooperative, and the enterprise system into a cooperative system. Workers would fare unequally in diverse enterprises-cooperatives, so that the next step would most likely be the introduction of national cooperation implemented directly by nationalization (take-over by the state) of private enterprises.

The forced inclusion of an alien element, which must necessarily lead to subversion of the existing system, is tantamount to a revolution. The revolution therefore need not immediately abolish the existing system and replace it with another. It can accomplish this as well through gradual transformation by means of such alien element.

It is possible however to apply the principles of a noncapitalist economic system to a segment of the population, incomes, returns, prices, etc., provided that the fundamental organizational principle of capitalism is thereby not negated. For example, the state may tax enterprise income to serve its solidarist purposes (a solidarist contribution based on capacity to pay) but it cannot tax away the entire income, because this would subvert the business enterprise system of production.

A state pursuing solidarist objectives may assume the exercise of care for entire sectors of the economy (by branches, or by individuals) and incorporate them in the solidarist sector that exists alongside or superimposed upon the nation's capitalist sector. Alternatively, it may intervene in the economy and its spontaneous order by compelling the economically strong to assist the economically weak, by erecting safeguards designed to protect the weak in the economic struggle, etc. A special case arises when the state, in pursuing its solidarist purposes, displaces equilibrium prices (prices in a broad sense, i.e., prices of goods, labor, money, and foreign exchange) and replaces their equilibrium function. This is known as the controlled economy and will be dealt with separately below.

And so we see that one can build on capitalist foundations, without destroying capitalism, a partial cooperative system, through cooperatives and public corporations, and one can also realize partial solidarism through public corporations and through legal norms compelling the economically strong to assist the economically weak.

VII. ECONOMIC SYSTEMS AND SYSTEMS OF ETHICS

Individualism and solidarism are two diametrically opposite systems through which nations exercise care to maintain and improve their lives. To each corresponds an appropriate order regulating the mutual conduct of members of national economic communities. Such order can take either the form of legal norms that involve compulsion, or ethical norms that do not.

When everyone exercises care for his own welfare there exist only negative relationships among individuals, not positive ones. An individual does not assist another when each is responsible only for his own welfare. Nevertheless, even then there must exist an order governing the behavior of self-responsible individuals so that conflicts are avoided, so that no one infringes upon another's person (libel, bodily harm) or property (theft, robbery). Only when this is so will all be able to exercise the best possible care for their welfare. E.g., the rule that everyone must drive on the right minimizes collisions and maximizes everyone's freedom of movement. As a result, there have developed, over the millenia, rules of mutual conduct, legal norms and ethical precepts among men responsible for their own welfare. Ethical precepts are norms by which we judge behavior to be moral, honest, just, decent; or else immoral, dishonest, etc. A set of ethical precepts (legal norms will be discussed below) forms a moral code which is a set of rules addressed to the citizens who are guided by it and who judge their behavior in accordance with it. On the other hand (from the viewpoint of the formation of such precepts) it is a set of purposive rules (a purposive code). To the individualistic and solidarist economic systems correspond two moral codes which are correspondingly diametrical opposites: the individualistic and solidarist moral codes.

To understand these two moral codes, we must inquire what is their meaning, i.e., what purpose they serve. What may be the purpose of the individualistic moral code? The ban against theft, robbery, bodily harm, etc., benefits all, but especially those unable to fend for themselves, i.e., the weak. Hence, the individualistic moral code secures for the weak–and hence for everyone–the opportunity to exercise care to maintain and improve their lives as best they can. The strong are therefore charged only with the negative duty not to do in, destroy, or infringe upon the weak. They have no *positive* obligation to assist them, as they do in the solidarist moral code. Moral categories, such as honesty, justice, virtue, etc., are formulated in accordance with the moral code. An honest man does not steal, does not commit fraud, does not violate contracts, does not infringe upon another's property, and he has come by his property without theft, fraud, etc. A just man fulfills his contractual obligations, and he is considerate where property of others is concerned. Self-responsibility is a merit and a virtue. The principles of the individualistic ethic, which express the mutual relationships among men negatively, are codified in the Ten Commandments ("Thou shalt not steal" "Thou shal not kill," etc.).

Even though this moral code gives to everyone, including the weak, an opportunity to develop as best they can, it by no means guarantees evenly balanced development of the collective, and hence the continuous and ideal development of the collective social body. Capitalist individualism implies economic struggle among men, because every contract represents economic struggle, which becomes system-wide through competition. In this struggle, the economically strong are more likely to emerge victorious than the economically weak. Whereas workers are motivated to agree to offer their labor because of concern about their livelihood and the livelihood of their families, the employers who hire them are motivated by the desire to increase their returns, compared to what they would earn by work alone. The ethic of individualism is, primarily, the ethic of the capitalist struggle. However, within its framework there evolve gradually such ideas as the "just" wage, the injustice of property income ("he who does not work, neither shall he eat"), and the notion that cooperation should replace the capitalist struggle and abolish man's subservience to man. This is the cooperative ethic. Nevertheless, it is still an individualistic ethic and it contains no part of the solidarist ethic.

The solidarist ethic corresponds to the solidarist economic system. It is embodied in the key principle of love of one's neighbor, the principle that goods ought to go to those who need them most, that the interests of the individual should be subordinate to those of the collective (country, nation, mankind, etc.). This imparts a different meaning to concepts such as justice and virtue, as we explain below. However, all solidarist norms are postulates that follow teleologically from the purpse of maintaining and improving the life, health and culture of the nation or of mankind (depending on who is included in the solidarist community, in the love of one's neighbor). From this purpose follows appropriate action, namely assignment of work in accordance with capacity and distribution of goods in accordance with need, positive assistance of the strong to the weak, and human relationships based on the maxim: "Thou shalt love they neighbor as thyself." I do not love my neighbor as myself if I keep more than I need while he is in need. All the principles of the solidarist ethic derive from the purpose of pursuing the ideal of life, health and culture of the nation or mankind.

A postulate is a postulate vis-a-vis a superior purpose; from the viewpoint of a subordinate individual, it is a norm. Every ethical norm thus has its purposive superstructure, and each system of ethics that regulates an order of interpersonal relationships is a purposive realization of that order's desideratum. The solidarist ethic realizes the ideal of life, health and culture of the nation (mankind), i.e., its development toward this ideal, a development which is *balanced* because that is the best way to make certain that it is permanent. This then is the desideratum which the solidarist ethic seeks to realize.

Behavior is morally good when it conforms to an ethical norm. But, when we say that an ethical norm realizes a desideratum, we mean that it realizes a desideratum derived from the purpose served by the norm (as postulate). We can see now that the ethical norms of love of one's neighbor is an element of the whole system which is above all purposive.

The evolution, over millenia, of ethical norms regulating the order of personal interrelationships is not accidental. It proceeds in the direction best suited to safeguard everyone's life.

But as we saw, various ethical norms do not constitute a single system. Individualistic and solidaristic ethical norms cannot be combined in a single system. The former impose on the strong only the negative duty not to destroy the weak; the latter impose on them the positive duty to assist them (work in accordance with capacity, enjoyment according to objective need). Protection of private property (honesty means not to steal) is an element of the individualistic moral code, whereas private property is unacceptable in the solidarist ethic, (Proudhon: "La propriete c'est le vol"). The purpose of the individualistic ethic is to enable everyone, including the weak, to pursue happiness undisturbed (Bentham: "The greatest happiness of the greatest number"). It is an expression of the individual's will to live. The purpose of the solidarist ethic is the ideal of the nation's life, health, and culture–an expression of the whole society's will to live. Private, subjective welfare stands opposed to public, objective welfare. From the viewpoint of the former, the collective exists to serve the individual; from the viewpoint of the latter, the role of the individual is to serve the collective. In the former case, the role of the state is to safeguard and improve the individual's life; in the latter, the state (society) takes precedence and the role of the individual is to serve the state. Hillel, the Pharisee ("Do not unto others that which is hateful unto thee"), and the Ten Commandments ("Thou shalt not kill") stand opposed to Jesus ("Thou shalt love thy neighbor as thyself").

Moral codes thus become opposites, as do the systems for the exercise of care to maintain and improve life. "Justice" and "morality" have no specific content as such, unless we specify which particular code of ethics we have in mind. When we speak of the "just price" or the "just wage", we have in mind the individualistic ethic. When we speak of justice as assistance given to those who need it most, we have in mind the solidarist ethic. One cannot bridge and unify these opposing ethical systems; one can only superimpose one on the other. And so it is clear that each ethical system has its purposive superstructure and that it is an order, with respect to this superstructure.

The polarity of ethical systems can be outlined as follows:

Ethical System

(a) Individualistic	(b) Solidarist
1. negative norms	1. positive norms
2. the strong should not infringe upon and exploit the weak	2. the strong should assist the weak

The cooperative ethic is clearly an individualistic ethic. And this is in agreement with our classificatory schema of economic systems.

VIII. THE MORAL NATURE OF MEN AND ECONOMIC SYSTEMS

By moral nature of men we understand here their dominant propensity to live and act in accordance with one of the ethical systems. It would be a rare man who would lack any shred of compassion for others, and it would be an equally rare man who would never consider his own interest. That is why we speak of a *dominant* propensity to act one way or another.

The moral nature of man results, on one hand, from his native instinct and, on the other, from the impact of education aimed at guiding or altering his native instinct. We must also distinguish permanent tendencies from passing enthusiasm or excitement. In a flare of enthusiasm, even very selfish men are capable of great sacrifices for their fellow men and for society as a whole.

Men who think only of their own interest and have no compassion with others (or society) are called egoists. Those who have compassion with their fellow men (or society) and act accordingly are called altruists. Egoists do not tend to live in accordance with the solidarist ethic. But this does not necessarily mean that they tend to live in accordance with the individualistic ethic. Their egoism may be so ruthless that they find themselves opposed to any moral code whatsoever. Nevertheless, a rational egoist admits—in his own interest—the need for the individualistic ethic and for conduct in accordance with it, because it enables him to act as he wishes ("Do not unto others that which is hateful to thee").

In this sense, we are justified to say that egoists can live in accordance with the individualistic but not the solidarist ethic. Were they to live in accordance with the solidarist ethic, they could not follow their own wishes. Altruism means primarily compassion with one's fellow-man, but this always includes both—the person with whom I have compassion and myself—within a higher entity. I see him as a brother, as member of the nation or of mankind. To act in accordance with subjective utility is not the same as to act selfishly because it is logically necessary that I always act in accordance with subjective utility, even when I derive enjoyment from assisting my fellow-man.

Those who advocate economic solidarism are not always altruists. Often the reason why some people are advocates of solidarism is the egoism of the weak, because they expect assistance from the strong, but have no altruistic feelings whatsoever for the strong or for anyone else. Egoism can therefore be an obstacle to economic solidarism (as far as the strong are concerned), or a motive for bringing it about (as far as the weak are concerned).

For the egoists, the solidarist ethic is a moral code for which they may occasionally feel great enthusiasm, but which they do not follow—as a rule—in the conduct of their lives. One would expect them to be suited to live in accordance with the individualistic rather than the solidarist ethic. But both ethics are also realized in the form of the corresponding economic systems. Egoists are suited to live in and implement the individualistic economic system. They are not suited to implement solidarism. If all men became perfect altruists they would live spontaneously and voluntarily in solidarism (e.g., the early Christians were communists).

This means that a particular economic system will arise freely and spontaneously, provided it corresponds with the moral nature of the citizens. On the other hand, a system (we have in mind solidarism) must be implemented—in whole or in part—through compulsion when implemented among individuals who are not solidarists. Men do not feel that a rule constrains their will and freedom, if they desire the same thing as the rule does. The norm "Thou shalt not kill" does not constrain one's freedom if one has no desire to commit murder. So, if solidarism does not agree with the moral nature of mean, it can only be implemented through compulsion, at the expense of liberty.

There can be no doubt that egoism has been, heretofore, the dominant tendency of all men. But it is certain that the awareness and the feeling of solidarity are on the increase. This is associated with social development (technical and economic progress, increased dependence of the individual upon society, luxury alongside poverty) and re-education. But it is not clear whether all this is sufficient to suppress egoism which appears to be the result of the instinct of self-preservation. It is not even possible to await the outcome of the re-education process, and it is necessary to implement the agreed upon degree of solidarism through compulsion. E.g., the entire system of taxation is a solidarist feature in the state economy implemented through legal compulsion.

Another question is whether solidarism can be successfully implemented on a permanent basis, in view of the fact that all labor in solidarism is compulsory (both the kind and the amount) and that all consumption, including the limits of consumption, is mandatory. Compulsion cannot replace material interest as the motivating force of progress. We do not claim that there would be no individuals in solidarist society who would not perceive their interest only as selfish gain, but as the benefit of society as a whole. Such men, guided by their self-less motives, would be capable of great things. But this is also true of capitalism: the greatest ideas were not motivated by prospect of monetary gain. However what we have in mind is the average man in the business of everyday life. It is for this reason that the individualistic system, particularly capitalism, is seen as more efficient, i.e., superior with respect to productivity. But when the body politic is threatened and must perform at maximum capacity—as in wartime—men resort to solidarism. The desire to be free is solidarism's greatest adversary.

IX. ECONOMIC ORDER AND LEGAL ORDER

The activity which we attribute to the state is its policy. The state conducts policy by enacting legal norms (legal order) and by operating the state sector of the economy. This is like a father exercising control over his children by directives and prohibitions while feeding and clothing them in his economy. The two activities combine to form a whole; they are two aspects of state activity. For example, the state may direct parents to provide their children's education, or it may provide for it in public schools. Only when we consider both aspects do we obtain a complete picture of the relevant state activity.

The state's position is different in different economic systems. In pure individualistic capitalism it may not participate in economic activity, though it may own business enterprises (state capitalism). As for the enactment of legal norms the state's function is analogous to that of the moral code. It issues rules and regulations to minimize conflict; it enacts traffic regulations–literally as well as figuratively–: Drive on the right! Do not violate anyone's control of his goods! Do not encroach on his rights! Observe standardized contracts!* Do not physically harm or libel anyone! All this benefits in particular the weak vis-a-vis the strong. In individualistic capitalism the state assumes a negative stance, vis-a-vis the economy and this applies also to the legal order. The state's role in pure individualistic capitalism used to be described as purely legal, and the only function of the law was thought to be maintenance of order in a negative sense. The state used to be described therefore in the literature as *the legal state.* (Speaking ironically, Lassalle compared the role of the capitalist state with the function of a "night watchman".)

In pure national cooperation the state's function vis-a-vis households is the same as the function of the capitalist state vis-a-vis *all* economic units, i.e., it is limited to "traffic regulation", to protection in a negative sense. The cooperative state carries on production in state establishments and—as subject under the law—requires at least as much protection against theft, robbery, damage, sabotage, etc., as does a private producer. The mutual relationship of workers and state establishments calls for arrangements that are different from the free and unrestricted collective bargaining contracts in capitalism. Protection of state establishments does not serve the interests only of a few but the interests of all, since all are employed by them. It serves the *common* interest. Common interest takes precedence over the interests of individuals. It represents the general interest of all in some matter, and it takes therefore precedence over a single individual's interest in that matter. *Common* interest (of all individuals) must be distinguished from the interest of the collective which only appears in solidarism, and which we shall refer to as *public* interest. (The "collective" and "all individuals" are not identical.)

In pure solidarism the state is the only economic decision maker. Therefore all of the exercise of care directed toward the ideal of a nation's life, health, and culture goes on within the state economy. The state has control of all goods, it produces them and uses them in its economy. It requires a body of laws to protect its economy (its control of goods, the functioning of its economy) against all harm (damage, theft, sabotage, etc.). Laws are also needed, to delimit the duties of citizens, as objects of state care, e.g., concerning work in accordance with capacity, and consumption in accordance with objective need. Finally, laws are required

---

* By standardizing contracts for commercial relations (in civil and commercial law) the state "lays the rails" for "economic traffic."

to regulate the behavior and duties of solidarist state organs engaged in valuation and economic decision making on the state's behalf.

The interests protected here by legal obligations are those of the collective and must be distinguished from the common interests of all individuals. E.g., the treatment of a patient in the solidarist state is in the interest of the collective or—if you wish—in the interest of the state as agent of the solidarist economy. But it is not in the interest of the patient—at least his interest is not decisive for the nature and method of the treatment. The interest of the collective is not the sum of the interests of individuals associated in the body politic. It cannot be the sum of these interests because it does not coincide, in any way, with private interests. What is decisive is the collective's gain or loss of life, health and culture, and the loss of an individual's life may be outweighed by another's gain in culture, and vice versa. We refer to the interest of the collective as *public* and distinguish it from *common* interest (common to all individuals) and *private* interest (of separate individuals).

The set of all norms having legal force in a state forms its legal order. We may consider such order from the viewpoint of subordinate subjects (individuals submitting to duties and obligations) who look to the legal norms and inquire: "What are we to do?" They inquire as to their duties, and if the interests of some individuals are covered and protected, those individuals also inquire if their rights, their interests—as correlates of their duties—are protected. This is the normological view which tells us what has legal force, what is right according to the law, etc. As Weyr says, the validity of a norm derives from the validity of another norm, and the validity of all norms derives from the constitution.

We may also view the legal order from the standpoint of the norm-creating agent—the state—who enacts norms as expressions of its will, as its postulates. The state enacts them as instruments (means) for the realization of its ends, and we must therefore understand and interpret legal norms in this way if we take the state's point of view. Here all means and ends combine to form an order. It is only from this viewpoint that the legal order is an order, and it can only be a purposive order. From this viewpoint we observe neither right nor validity (which apply only in relation to a norm). What we observe is the purposive and systemic nature of norms or, better still, of the postulates which the norms express.

When the state is neither purely capitalist, cooperative, or solidarist, and when elements of economic solidarism are superimposed on a capitalist foundation, either in the state sector (e.g., tax revenues and government expenditures), or in the form of some legal norm (e.g., imposition on the strong of obligations toward the weak), then the legal order no longer possesses uniform structure. The state is then not just a "traffic regulator" and guardian of order in a negative sense (the "legal state"), but over and above that, champion of solidarist interests and solidarist care. For this it requires solidarist norms (e.g., concerning tax liabilities, assistance of the strong to the weak, etc.). The legal order is then no longer uniform. But this is not to say that it is a random assortment of norms. If we wish to establish whether it is an order (system) and what sort of order, we must consider it from the standpoint of the agent of will (the state) who issues norms as its directives and prohibitions–i.e., teleologically–not from the standpoint of the subordinate subjects, i.e., normologically.

It is then apparent that in that case legal norms tend toward two distinct systemic centers, that we have here a mixture of two different systems, individualism and solidarism. From time immemorial it was always felt that legal norms had this dual character, that one type (civil law, commercial law, etc.) constituted private law, corresponding to individualism, while another type constituted public law, corresponding to solidarism. The difference between public and private law cannot be discerned from the normological viewpoint (of subordinate subjects). From that viewpoint we can only discern duties rather than the protected interests around which duties are erected as their negative imprints. Only when we trace–from the teleological standpoint–the purpose pursued in enacting the norms and the interests (disiderata) that the norms protect cane we perceive this difference, this dualism of two purposive centers to which the norms tend and around which they purposively concentrate.

A legal order constituted in this complex fashion for the purpose of implementing two distinct economic (and ethical) systems, lacks a uniform concept of justice. And the statement that the law ought to be just is devoid of meaning, unless we specify what concept of justice we have in mind (depending on the economic or ethical system). Otherwise, we would have to define justice as conformance with the legal order. But that would only be a formal definition.

X. THE THEORY OF THE STATE ECONOMY AS A PROBLEM OF ECONOMIC SYSTEMS

Since the economies of the real world are mixed economies, we must first establish—with respect to each phenomenon that we wish to explain—to which economic system, and hence which system of phenomena, it belongs. This follows from the fact that phenomena are explained by their relationship to systems. This holds a fortiori when several systems, with several purposive (ordering) centers, meet in a single phenomenon. For example, to explain why workers work eight hours a day, one must first understand that it is in their subjective interest to keep working as long as their subjective relative cost (the disutility of a unit of labor) is less than their subjective relative utility (utility of the wage earned by a unit of labor). But it is not left to them to determine the duration of the work day, to keep working in accordance with their subjective valuation. The state cuts off the work day after eight hours, (legal regulation) because it pursues the solidarist objective of the nation's life, health and culture and accordingly values the utility of goods that would be produced during the ninth and subsequent hours less than the loss, the decrease of the workers' life and health, that would result from such work. Prior to the enactment of the legislation, the utility of the wage and disutility of each unit of labor were weighed by each worker on his scale of subjective valuation. It is now the state that weighs–on the scale of objective valu- (increase or decrease of life, health, and culture)–the objective utility of the goods produced (their importance for health, etc.) against the loss of the workers' health, etc. resulting from such production. And the state determines that the utility, in this sense, of the ninth hour of work falls short of the cost.

Here we have a junction of two economic systems, and the phenomenon is explained in terms of the two, each with its own system of valuation. This is always so when several economic systems meet, join or combine in some phenomenon or set of phenomena.

We consider now the state sector of the economy which we have chosen as the model from which we draw examples and cases of a junction of all three economic systems. All attempts to interpret it in a satisfactory manner have failed, as long as it was not interpreted teleologically, as a purposive complex, and as long as it was not recognized that it was not a homogeneously purposive complex but a formation in which all three economic systems meet. To understand the state sector is to explain how each of its elements tends to its purposive center, and that this includes every element.

At its present stage of development the state sector is far from homogeneous. It is not adequate to define it as the income and expenditures of public authorities (Dalton). If a shoemaker's household and workshop (enterprise) were combined and he kept a single set of income-and-expenditure accounts, this would not be a homogenous economy, though the same agent was involved. An economy is a system and a homogeneous economy is a homogeneous system. This is far from being so with respect to state income and expenditures where the latter include–in addition to other expenditures–the expenditures of state enterprises. Revenues include tax revenues, sales revenues of state enterprises, and various fees and charges.

The state sector consists of several types of economic units and establishments that must be distinguished from the systemic point of view. It is not difficult to distinguish state enterprises from the rest of the state sector, but it is difficult to distinguish solidarist and cooperative elements within the non-enterprise part of the sector because they mutually permeate each other. Analysis shows the following:

1. The *Solidarist nucleus* of the state sector. We are not concerned here with pure solidarism but with partial solidarism built on a capitalist or cooperative foundation. The solidarist nucleus obtains what it needs from subordinate capitalist economies (households and enterprises) or cooperative economies (cooperatives). Such economies contribute according to their capacity (minimization of cost) and their contributions are taxes. The purpose of the state sector is to realize the ideal of the nation's life, health and culture. Hence an increase in the nation's life, health and culture represents an increase in utility, and a decrese represents a cost. When a contribution, a tax, is to be levied on households with different incomes, it will be levied on those for whom a lower post-tax income represents a lesser decrease of life, health and culture. Ceteris paribus this will be households with higer income. As more taxes are gradually imposed, this leads to higher incomes being taxed so much that they tend to the same post-tax level as lower incomes, i.e., to income equalization. Expressed in percentage terms it implies a steep progressivity of the tax system. This involves consideration of the disutility of taxes, of direct costs, from the solidarist viewpoint. But we must not forget that here the solidarist state sector represents only partial solidarism, an adjunct of the private capitalist, and/or cooperative, economy. Hence we must also consider the harm to the functioning of the economy which such taxation will cause. If the taxes were to impair the future functioning of the economy the damage (the cost of the tax) would include not only the direct present cost, but also the indirect cost resulting from the impairment of the operation of the operation of the capitalist economy. Future income formation and thus the basis of self-responsible care by individuals to maintain and improve their lives would be impaired or destroyed. We shall refer to the capacity to contribute, when measured by direct cost, as *personal* capacity and when measured by indirect cost, as *material* capacity to contribute. In our case the point of view of personal capacity to contribute led to equalization of incomes. Suppose that all incomes in excess of 100,000 crowns were taxed away. The affected income recipients would then have no motiva-

tion to earn income (work, production) in excess of this figure. No one would therefore earn a pre-tax income in excess of 100,000 crowns. The solidarist economy would then be forced to lower the income bracket, and the same result would follow, until the business enterprise system of production broke down completely. Consideration of this indirect effect (impact upon the capitalist foundation of the economy) has led to such progressivity of the tax structure which leaves to taxpayers in higher brackets after-tax incomes higher than the after-tax incomes of taxpayers in lower brackets. Income equalization which has destructive effects is ruled out. The tax structure is thus an outcome of both *personal* and *material* capacity to contribute.

Tax revenue is used to finance purchases of goods and services which the solidarist sector acquires for society as a whole, or for the economically weak, and which it distributes without charge (the so-called principle of pure government expenditures). Expenditures are made in accordance with objective utility or objective need. The boundary of rationality lies at the point where relative utility derived from spending tax revenues no longer exceeds relative cost (loss) resulting from paying taxes. It represents the limit of available resources, a minimum income that is not to be taxed.

In addition to *personal* solidarity (union of the strong and the weak for the purpose of allocating both the burdens and the fruits of labor) such economy also realizes *material* solidarity of various ends included in the ideal of life, health, and culture. One should not continue to satisfy a need if another need yields relatively more utility, and this implies interdependence of all ends and the carrying of the satisfaction of all ends to the point of equalization of relative marginal utilities. This aspect of the state sector represents therefore a genuine and a complete economy sui generis, one whose systemic order is totally different from the other economic activities of the state.

2. *Cooperative establishments.* Another type of state activity (including activity of public bodies such as municipalities, etc.) consists of providing to the citizens goods and services at cost, against payments known as *rates* (this resembles the practice of cooperatives). E.g., an individual may get his own water; water may be supplied by a private corporation at a price that yields a profit; or else a cooperative may be

established to provide water at cost (water rate). The function of the cooperative may be taken over by a municipality without changing the water rate. These activities of municipalities, and other public bodies including central government, are cooperative. They are carried on by cooperative establishments, not business enterprises. These establishments are not business enterprises because their purpose is not profit maximization, and the rates they charge, the cooperative payments, do not include profit. They are not solidarist economies because they do not distribute goods and services to the citizens without charge, according to objective need, but to all who demand them, for a payment. Even security services can be cooperatively procured, and payments that cover costs can be made on a lump-sum basis (not for each service separately) in accordance with the protected interest (e.g., a watchman may be paid by farmers in accordance with the number of plum trees that he guards). The payment is not a tax, even if it is proportionate to income or net return. This is the case of the "legal state" which merely performs for the capitalist sector the cooperative protection of property, of incomes, or net revenues (the function of the "night watchman"!) in return for lump-sum payments that are not based on capacity to pay. A *tax* is a solidarist contribution based on capacity to pay (where there is no quid pro quo); a *rate* is a cooperative price of a good or service (a cost price without profit) set on an individual or lump-sum basis (e.g., tuition). Taxes are an aspect of solidarism in the state sector, whereas rates are an aspect of cooperative establishments.

Within the state sector may also be found a combination of solidarism and cooperation. This occurs when less than full-cost price is charged for services performed and the deficit is covered from solidarist contributions. Consider, e.g., a municipal bath operated on the cooperative principle, which implies a cooperative price, a charge for using the bath. But the charge may be rather high, so that it discourages many from making use of the bath. The municipality, in its capacity of agent of solidarist care interested in the citizens' health, may take the position that it would be desirable to lower the charge and thus expand the number of those using the bath. The result would be a deficit not covered by the charge. To the degree that the charge covers cost, it is a cooperative establishment, to the degree that it does not, it is solidarist. It is also possible (with similar intent) to charge graduated fees, according to the wealth or income of those who demand the service, that is, to some extent, on the basis of ability to pay. But this is not a tax, because those who pay such charges receive services based on their subjective wants. When charges are graduated, there may even be cases when they exceed the cost price and, to that extent they become taxes.

An example of administration of payments is a *fund* (an institution), which is a cooperative analogue of business enterprise. It collects payments to be used only for the benefit of contributors; e.g., a fund to maintain and reconstruct highways financed from contributions of highway users. In transitional cases it is not always possible to distinguish these two aspects from the budgetary viewpoint, though they are aspects of two entirely different systems.

3. *Enterprises.* The state and other public bodies may operate profit-making enterprises producing goods and services for the market exactly as do private corporations, i.e., for everyone willing to pay the price. Prices include profit. State enterprises are therefore part of the capitalist system, they represent state capitalism.

The important question is, why does the state establish (or take over) and operate its own enterprises? One must reject the view that it raises in this manner revenue for its solidarist activities because such source of revenue would be quite inappropriate from the solidarist viewpoint. The state solidarist sector collects contributions from the citizens based on their ability to pay, in accordance with its objective and mission. And profits of state enterprises do not at all correspond to this. Consequently, it is methodologically incorrect to lump together profits of state enterprises, with other state revenues. State enterprises perform a function for buyers of their goods and services which is analogous to the function performed by cooperative establishments, the only difference being that state enterprises include in the price which they charge an additional amount (enterprise profit), which is not included in the price charged by cooperative establishments. It is therefore inconsistent to include, as part of state revenue, the total charges of state establishments which correspond to cooperative prices but to include only the excess of price over cost in the case of state enterprises. Consistency would then require that cooperative charges should be excluded from state revenue altogether.*

Another possible rationale for the existence of state enterprise can be that the state as entrepreneur may behave differently than a private businessman, in that it may be satisfied with lower net returns than it could earn, by charging lower prices, paying higher wages, etc. It is because of these considerations that state enterprises are public enterprises which may be transformed–if the public interest becomes more pronounced–into cooperative establishments. Both cooperative establishments and state enterprises sell goods and services to all willing to pay the price or rate.

One more step and we are in an altogether different systemic order, solidarism, where goods and services are distributed to all according to objective need, without payment, and where citizens contribute according to their capacity, though they may get no goods or services from the establishment in which they serve.

Any industrial branch may be transferred from the private to the state sector (etatism), but this in itself is not decisive as far as the economic system is concerned. As noted earlier, footwear used to be produced [in Czechoslovakia] by Bata capitalistically through private enterprise. Assume that the state takes over the production of footwear. It can produce, firstly, in the same way as did Bata, in state enterprises, producing what the consumers prefer, what they subjectively want and for what they are therefore willing to pay the listed price, including profit. Secondly, the state may transform the enterprises into cooperative establishments by lowering prices and abolishing profit, but otherwise continue producing what consumers prefer, what they subjectively desire, as long as they pay the cooperative price. The state may finally change the care for the nation's footwear into solidarist care. It may not produce what the consumers prefer, but what it itself decides is objectively beneficial for them (for their health), what they objectively need. This will be

---

* It is only at a lower level of social and economic development, when the state is as yet unable to tax money incomes and enterprise revenues of its citizens, that income from state assets (e.g., crown lands, etc.) pays for state needs, military expenditures, etc.

allocated to them free of charge (e.g., a pair of winter boots, a pair of summer sandals, one shoe for one-legged people, etc.). The costs will be recovered from the citizens in taxes. (It is possible that an individual who gets no shoes—perhaps because he is bed-ridden—will pay the most.)

We observe therefore, that not all activities included in the state sector constitute a homogeneous economy, but that they are a systemically quite heterogeneous collection of activities consisting of numerous enterprises and establishments plus a solidarist sector. In this way the exposition of economic systems helped us to explain and to understand the structure of the state sector.

XI. THE CONTROLLED ECONOMY AS A SPECIAL PROBLEM

1. Introduction

We discuss the controlled economy toward the end of this study, because to understand it fully requires prior understanding of all the relationships of economic systems. The controlled economy came into being in World War I. The Commercial Code of Austria-Hungary authorized the political magistrate of the first instance to fix prices of the necessities of daily life. This authorization came to be widely used during World War I. As shortages of grain products and other goods developed, the first step taken was to set maximum prices. However, maximum prices by themselves, though they helped to combat profiteering, could not mitigate physical shortages. Given the shortages, prices would have climbed to equilibrium levels. Without price controls they would have reached levels at which available stocks plus current production would have been sufficient for buyers able and willing to pay such prices. Higher prices would have depressed demand—primarily, of course, demand of the less affluent—so that shortages, e.g., the shortage of bread, would have impacted upon the least affluent, because the wealthy would not have cared how high the price of bread was, and thus would not have suffered.

But maximum prices as such could not help. With a lower controlled price the poor could continue buying bread, but since not enough was available, it became necessary to limit the consumption of all. Also, producers were unwilling to sell bread at the low price. And so the result of every new price ceiling was the disappearance of the good from the market because price had lost its allocative function, and nothing was put in its place. This was soon recognized, and the former dual function of prices (to call forth production and to restrict consumption) was therefore replaced by state compulsion: producers were compelled to make deliveries while consumers' purchases and consumption were restricted by rationing. However, restrictions imposed on consumers were not all the same but were differentiated according to objective need, i.e., seen from the solidarist viewpoint. E.g., special rations were issued to those performing heavy work, or to children.

The same approach came to be used after the war in the foreign exchange market. The limited supply of foreign exchange was rationed, and in order to strengthen the exchange rate only the most important payments abroad were permitted, (foreign-exchange permit procedure).

The concept of controlled economy was further worked out in Germany, prior to World War II, in connection with the drive toward autarky. Subsequently, during the war, it was introduced everywhere and became the economic program of German National Socialism. It involved not only restrictions of prices, wages, interest rates, duties, etc. (but the replacement of the equilibrium functions of prices in the capitalist system by the solidarist principle). An individual willing and able to buy a good may not be allowed to, but one whose use of the good is seen as most important, from the viewpoint of the collective, may be allowed to do so. The state becomes the solidarist regulator of capitalism.

To fully understand the controlled economy, we must have a good understanding of the equilibrium function of prices (in a broad sense) in capitalism. We must therefore devote somewhat more attention to this question than we did earlier in describing the capitalist system.

2. The equilibrium function of prices in capitalism

The capitalist economic system is based on prices (in a broad sense). Prices guide production and consumption, they guide the allocation of labor and capital, they regulate who buys what, and they determine the distribution of income. They are formed in four markets:

a) prices of goods are formed in the goods market;
b) the price of labor, the wage rate, is formed in the labor market;
c) the price of using money, the rate of interest, is formed in the financial capital market;
d) the exchange rate is formed in the foreign exchange market, the market for instruments of foreign payments.

Prices of goods are said to be determined by supply and demand and by cost of production. However, supply and demand are themselves price-determined. To every price corresponds some quantity supplied and demanded; the price calls forth some volume of production and restricts the demand for the good. But neither supply and demand, nor cost of production determine price. No one likes to sell below his costs, but price is not determined by the fact that a certain cost was incurred to produce a good. On the contrary, one can incur the cost of producing a good because one can sell it at a price that covers the cost.

Price balances production and consumption. A falling price indicates disequilibrium, because at the old price consumption was too low, given the production which the price called forth. A rising price indicates disequilibrium at the old price for the opposite reason. Price fluctuations indicate that a new equilibrium price is being sought. Price therefore determines who shall produce how much of what (depending on relative costs), who shall buy how much of what (depending on relative utilities), and what cost the producer is willing to incur to produce the good. A detailed discussion of relative prices of different goods and of the absolute price level of all goods (which is related to money) can be found in Volume I of my *Soustava národního hospodářství [System of National Economy]*, 1938.

The above describes the situation that prevails in purely competitive markets, because cartellization—which excludes pure competition—leads to fixing or displacement of equilibrium prices (this will be discussed below). Prices are formed analogously in the other markets (prices in the broad sense: wage rates, interest rates, and foreign exchange rates), i.e., by balancing the factors which generate prices in the market. The interest rate balances capital supplied and demanded, the wage rate balances labor supplied and demanded, and the exchange rate balances payments to foreigners and payments from abroad. Each of these prices shapes the corresponding supply and demand to bring about equilibrium. The process will be explained further by using as example the foreign exchange rate.

One who exports goods for foreign currency must exchange the proceeds of his sales for domestic currency in the foreign exchange market. How much his proceeds will be depends on the exchange rate. This amounts to the same thing as if he sold the goods at home, and the domestic price rose or fell. It pays him to produce and export more if the price (the exchange rate) rises, and the converse is true if it falls. On the other hand, one who imports goods and who requires foreign currency to pay for them, will have to pay more in domestic currency if the exchange rate of the foreign currency rises, and vice versa. It is the same as if he bought in the home market and the price of the good rose—he would then reduce his purchases. Consequently, to each exchange rate corresponds some flow of payments abroad and payments from abroad (to be concise I consider here only payments on current account). When the exchange rate of foreign currency, expressed in domestic currency, (or of domestic currency expressed foreign currency) either rises or falls it is an unmistakable sign that the old rate was not an equilibrium rate, and that it is seeking a level that would restore equilibrium in the balance of payments.

And so the balance of production and consumption, of capital funds demanded and supplied, of labor demanded and supplied, and of payments to and from foreign countries, is associated in capitalism with four equilibria, with equilibrium prices (in a broad sense) that emerge in four markets: the goods market, the labor market, the capital market, and the foreign exchange market.

However, the equilibria in particular markets—and this must be particularly emphasized in an exposition of the controlled economy—are not independent of each other; on the contrary, they are interdependent. The price levels in the various markets are mutually dependent, and so are price changes. Price levels pass through a business enterprise as through a piece of crystal, and a particular price relationship motivates the enterprise to expand or contract its activity, since it determines its profitability. When prices of the goods produced by the enterprise are falling, this exercises pressure on profits and on the motivation and ability to employ capital and pay interest, to employ labor and pay wages. Decreased profitability due to lower prices releases capital and labor from enterprises, whereas rising prices stimulate enterprise motivation to hire more labor and borrow more capital funds. Similarly, the pressure of interest rates influences prices, wages, etc. If a certain configuration of prices (in a broad sense, i.e., prices of goods, interest rates, wage rates, and possibly exchange rates) tends to increase or decrease enterprise activity, this leads to shifts of equilibria in the corresponding markets. Disequilibrium and change in one market causes disequilibria in other markets. Hence, there can be no equilibrium in one market unless there is equilibrium in all markets. Changes in economic variables, such as consumption, production, harvests, the flight of capital from the country, etc., always keep on bringing about changes in some market, and price fluctuations keep on restoring equilibrium in the national economy as a whole (all this, of course, under competitive conditions).

3. The allocative (regulatory) function of prices in capitalism

Prices not only maintain the equilibrium order among their market determinants (production, consumption, etc.), but at the same time they determine the allocation of goods and the distribution of income. With given incomes and given subjective valuation, price determines the set of goods that the consumers buy with their incomes. All incomes are generated in enterprises. It is there that the objective net revenue, created by the enterprise as a working team, is formed as the difference between the market-determined prices of goods produced and prices of goods used up in the process of production. This objective return is then divided —once again through the market mechanism—among workers, capitalists, and entrepreneurs, because entrepreneurs' profit, capitalists' interest, and workers' wages are market determined. And so the distribution of money income is determined by equilibrium market prices and so is the allocation of goods (given subjective valuation), because the structure of expenditures, with prices given, is such as to bring about maximum utility in return for the income spent.

Purchases of goods by enterprises (rather than purchases by households as consuming economic units) are also made according to relative utility. But they are not based on subjective utility (tastes, etc.) but on their usefulness to the enterprise, which is a function of the opportunity to make money. With given opportunities to make money (again a function of prices) the relative utility of goods bought by the enterprise rises as their prices fall, and falls as they rise. With given opportunities to make money, prices determine the quantity of goods bought by the enterprise, and the opportunity to make money is again a function of prices.

This describes the allocative (regulatory) function of prices—given a certain state of subjective valuation—since the composition of the set of goods which consumers buy with their incomes depends on prices and on subjective valuation. The relationship between subjective utility and price yields *relative* subjective utility, which determines purchases. It changes with a change of price or a change of subjective valuation. If goods were free, the consumer would make choices based only on utility, regardless of price (according to absolute utility). When goods are not free, he makes choices based on utility *and* prices (according to relative utility).

And so, prices and subjective valuation determine:

1. how the national product is allocated among industrial branches producing various goods, i.e., the volume of production of various goods;
2. the quantities of goods that can be acquired in the market by individual consuming units (households) and by individual money-making units (enterprises);
3. the amounts of funds obtained for consumption and for money-making purposes;
4. the amounts of labor acquired for the same purposes;
5. the quantities of means of foreign payments (foreign exchange) obtained.

All this is determined by prices (in a broad sense) and the corresponding markets.

4. Cartel prices no longer perform the market-clearing function but retain, in part, the allocative function

We have been concerned thus far with competitive prices. However, in the highest stage of the organizational development of capitalism, prices are also formed in an alternative way—by cartels. Sellers or buyers in a particular market agree among themselves not to compete against each other, but to demand or pay a certain price. Such agreements are possible in practice only when the number of sellers or buyers is not too large, and when the agreement—which must be of lasting duration—touches on a vital interest of theirs. Conceptually, such agreements may occur in any market. The agreements and the permanent organizations based on them are known as cartels (syndicates).

Conceptually, the following types of cartels are possible:

		A. Demand Side	B. Supply Side
I.	Goods market	impractical (too many consumers)*	production cartels**
II.	Labor market	employers' associations	employees' syndicates
III.	Capital market	impractical (too many debtors with different motives)	bank cartels
IV.	Foreign exchange	impractical because there are too many participants who come in and out of the market	

If a cartel does not face another cartel it dictates prices; if it does then prices are established by direct agreement (e.g., between employers' associations and employees' syndicates).***

---

* Consumers' cooperatives do not have the characteristics of cartels. They do not wish to displace prices and exclude competition. They wish to replace business enterprises; their objective is to exclude the element of profit from price.

** A production cartel may also act as a cartel in buying raw materials (a cartel of sugar refiners may administer sugar beet prices vis-à-vis a beet growers' association).

***Here we speak of *trade unions* or *industrial associations* because they are organized only among workers (and employers) belonging to the same trade, competing against one another, and capable of harming each other by competition. (Textile workers do not compete against steel workers.)

If cartels were satisfied with competitive equilibrium prices there would be no need for cartel agreements. But they want prices that are different, more advantageous to them. They wish to increase enterprise profits through higher prices or interest rates; workers wish to improve their living standards through higher wage rates, etc. It is thus private interest that motivates cartels to displace competitive equilibrium prices. The displacement of competitive equilibrium prices results in loss of their market-clearing function. If a cartel raises prices above the competitive level where there was balance of production and consumption, many producers will want to produce at these higher (profitable) prices, but few buyers will want to buy and consume. The cartel could not survive if it did nothing to restore balance, since the associated enterprises would rush into profitable production but would be unable to sell all their output. Accumulating inventories would push prices down and the cartel would break down. The cartel must therefore restrict production (establish quotas) and allocate the restricted output among its members. Cartel prices lose the market-clearing function and balance must be restored artifically (through quotas). They also lose—in part—the function of allocating production among enterprises (how much each enterprise will produce). This function too must be replaced by agreement (allocation of production quotas). But the cartel price continues to perform the allocative function vis-a-vis consumers. (Relative utility becomes a function of the cartel price.) But, when a cartel artificially replaces the market-clearing and allocative function by directive (agreement), it does so solely on the basis of profit considerations which have led to its being set up in the first place. The extent of the restriction of production follows simply from consideration of balance that is to be restored and maintained. But assignment of such restricted production to associated enterprises is not based on any valuation (purpose, importance); it is decided mechanically (allocation based on former shares of production). Here the cartel endeavors to restore the lost function of competitive price, but does so again solely on the basis of profit considerations.

However, cartel agreements may displace price from the equilibrium level without artifically replacing the lost market-clearing and allocative functions of competitive price. This occurs, e.g., in the case of agreements about working conditions between employers' associations and employees' syndicates (collective bargaining agreements, wage-schedule agreements).

If the negotiated price of labor exceeds the equilibrium price, it must lead to unemployment. But workers in search of work cannot be eliminated by trade unions in the same way that cartels can eliminate output through production quotas. The unions may set up unemployment benefit payments, but these are practical only for short-term unemployment, not for permanent displacement or for large-scale unemployment (ten workers can support an eleventh but two cannot support a third). The unemployed cannot go against the union wage scale, because it is also binding on the employers who cannot hire them at lower wage rates. The syndicate price loses its market-clearing function but retains the allocative function of placing labor in various jobs. But who is to get a job when supply does not equal demand? Workers want to control the manpower placement agencies to be able to control the placement of labor. But unemployment calls for state assistance, for solidarist help.

Price fixing by cartel agreements leads to price inflexibility. But we know that change in one market requires change and price adaptation in other markets if there is to be general equilibrium. Price fixing prevents such flexible adjustment, causing disturbances in the economy and disturbances of employment. For example, a balance of payments deficit causes capital to flow out of the country and interest rates to rise. If a stable exchange rate is desired, this requires downward adjustment of the price level and wage level; otherwise a recession will affect the enterprises. But this is prevented by cartel agreements about prices of goods and collective agreements about wage rates; these are rigid, and as a result the economy finds itself in a recession.

Finally—as we know—prices and subjective valuation determine how far the production of various goods proceeds. This is determined by relative prices. The equilibrium of production of different goods requires continuous adjustment of relative prices. (For details see my *Soustava národního hospodářství [System of National Economy]* Vol. 1, 1938). We may therefore speak of equilibrium relative prices. When the output of different goods is decided and fixed by cartels, this can lead to disruption of equilibrium in this sense as well.

5. The solidarist state finds capitalist allocation inappropriate for its purpose

It follows from what was said that allocation means allocation of production and of the national product among various outputs and allocation of goods among different consuming and money-making economic units, as well as allocation of labor, money capital, and foreign exchange among them. In capitalism allocation occurs simply in accordance with how much individuals are willing and able to pay.

In pure solidarism where the state pursues the ideal of the nation's life, health and culture it would organize the structure of production and the allocation of goods differently. Such state therefore regards capitalist allocation as inappropriate for its purpose. Indeed, at times that are critical for the nation's survival (defense, war), it finds capitalist allocation intolerable. However, it may not wish to establish pure solidarism, but only to alter capitalism, preserving the business enterprise system of production, while modifying all the above aspects of allocation, to bring it into harmony with solidarist interests and purposes.

There may be disagreement with the allocation of output and the guidance of resources to produce different goods which result when the allocative function is performed by prices and subjective valuation. E.g., there may be a greater need for food and necessities than for luxuries. When production of consumer goods is restricted, the solidarist state may not agree that it should be the object of price competition, so that those who are hurt most are primarily those who are least affluent, whereas the solidarist purpose may require that food should be allocated according to objective need. Allocation of raw materials, auxiliary materials, and machinery to enterprises, decided solely by price competition is not feasible either the state desires that they should be allocated to enterprises producing such goods and in such quantities as are in agreement with the solidarist valuation. Enterprises should not be permitted to get raw materials to produce luxuries when such production is restricted or prohibited in favor of necessities, defense goods, etc. By the same token, capitalist allocation of money capital and of labor, and their employment in production, is inappropriate when they should be employed to produce goods according to their importance as seen from the solidarist viewpoint.

Solidarist valuation may be appropriate even in normal times ("health before luxury"), but it is definitely applicable in times of war and national defense, when it becomes truly a matter of the nation's life and death. The nation's will to live is reflected in resolute solidarism.

The solidarist critique applies to the allocative function of competitive prices as well as cartel prices set at levels motivated by the private interest (to make money) of cartel members rather than in accordance with the desired solidarist criteria.

A capitalist state that wishes to participate in productive activity while pursuing the objectives of society as a whole (e.g., national defense) must enter markets for goods, capital, and labor to obtain what is required by bidding up prices. It thus raises the prices of the goods that it buys against itself, as well as all others who compete against it for goods, capital, and labor while pursuing their private ends.

6. The controlled economy has its origin in price intervention.

The controlled economy is born from defense and war or the preparation for war. Shortages of goods, capital, and foreign exchange in war time unleash competitive budding and lead to rising prices, which suppress demand, primarily the demand of those least able to pay. This means that the economically strong are made still stronger and the economically weak still weaker. It implies, e.g., that the brunt of food shortages is borne by the poor, that weaker enterprises succumb in the competitive struggle, etc. The state cannot stand by indifferently while this goes on. If during the war all people, including the very poor, risk their lives equally, it is unthinkable that one segment of the population should bear the brunt of scarcity and shortages brought on by the war, while another should live without suffering any deprivation, indeed in luxury (the solidarist viewpoint). Furthermore, profiteers make their appearance, calculating what the future will bring and profiting from the nation's scarcity and shortages.

The state has always intervened first in the sphere of prices by introducing prohibitions and punishments for profiteering, prohibitions to raise prices and interest rates, or by bringing in numerous ceilings on prices, interest rates, and exchange rates. Decrees that set maximum prices may have some effect on profiteering, but they fail to solve the real problem. Prices cease to be market-clearing. At such prices there are many people able and willing to buy, but there are shortages of goods and of producers willing to produce. Goods disappear from the market. The amount by which the natural equilibrium price exceeds the maximum price is made up in a variety of ways—personal acquaintanceship and nepotism, all sorts of bribes and barter. If people can get either cigarettes or butter some will trade butter for cigarettes (which are not available for money). Money simply tends to cease performing the function of medium of exchange, and barter is resorted to by those who comply with the decrees establishing price ceilings. Others make use of the *black market* (under-the-counter market). Prices there are much higher compared to what they would be under competitive conditions, because the market is narrower, restricted to those with greater purchasing power, and involving considerable risk of punishment.

Lowering interest rates and imposing ceilings on them results–given the shortages of loanable funds–in financial intermediaries restricting their credit to perfectly safe and riskless loans. And then it is favoritism, nepotism, and non-pecuniary factors that begin to play their role. There appear phenomena resembling barter in the goods market, i.e., direct dealings between capitalists and lenders, without the mediation of financial intermediaries.

In the foreign exchange market administrative setting of the exchange rate below the equilibrium level leads to a situation where foreign exchange earned in export trade is not sold to the central bank, but deposited abroad and sold illegally to domestic buyers who urgently require means to make foreign payments and cannot obtain them from the central bank, because they are in short supply. A black market in instruments of foreign payments emerges, and a parallel, higher exchange rate appears.

Analogous phenomena are not practical in the labor market because fixing the price of labor is not done to protect buyers (employers), and hence wage rates are not lowered relative to their equilibrium levels. Instead they are raised to protect the employees. *

7. The state replaces the lost market-clearing and allocative functions of administered prices

(a) The goods market.

In essense it is prices, as co-determinants of the volume of production of different goods, and of the quantities of goods, capital, etc., allocated

---

* Translator's note: The author refers here to minimum wages; but maximum wages are a distinct possibility in the "controlled economy."

to individual enterprises, that regulate the entire national economy. When they lose their market-clearing function, because of administrative price fixing, they also lose their allocative and regulatory function. The national economy loses its former automatic regulator, and nothing replaces it. Of course, this necessarily causes disruption, not to mention the fact that the solidarist objective–which is the point of departure for administrative price fixing–is not yet attained. If the state wishes to maintain the administered prices, it must provide a replacement not only for their market-clearing function but for their allocative function as well. It must restore balance in all markets and allocate–according to its own preferences–goods, capital, labor, and foreign exchange to economic units that wish to acquire them but whose demand cannot be fully satisfied at the administered prices.

Suppose that the state sets the price of some good, e.g., grain and flour, below equilibrium, so that many wish to buy, but none wish to sell at this price. The state must then bring first into balance the two determinants of price–production and consumption–by regulating the production and consumption of bread. It ascertains who the producers are and what their production possibilities are. It makes sure that the harvest is carried out, it enforces deliveries, it establishes feasible per capita consumption, in accordance with a given output, and it restricts demand by rationing bread.

Before prices were fixed, everyone simply adapted to them. Those who wanted, sold and milled grain, sold flour, and traded at the existing prices. On the other side of the market, those who wished bought as much grain and flour as they wanted. The state now enters as organizer on both sides of the market. It compels producers to join associations that possess knowledge about production and collect and distribute the product. In some branches of production some enterprises are shut down and only those that are sufficiently productive to be able to produce at the fixed price are allowed to operate. Production is concentrated, rationalized, etc. In this way the state proceeds from one branch of industry to another, organizing and rationalizing. It buys directly from the associations, on a priority basis and at the administered prices, what it requires for its purposes (e.g., grain for the army); then come other consumers, whose consumption is controlled to be in balance with production. Clearly, if quantities are insufficient to satisfy all who wish to buy at these prices–

be they households or enterprises–demand must be restricted. In all probability this will not be accomplished mechanically (e.g., everyone receiving one-third less) but by rationing (allocations) based on importance. For instance, with respect to household consumption, a distinction is made between adults, children, those doing heavy work and others, small children and the sick (special milk rations, etc.). Enterprises are classified into categories according to their importance as seen from the solidarist viewpoint, a higher category having priority in obtaining allocations over a lower category, or perhaps receiving larger allocations. Rations may be set in a general way, e.g., household food rations, or individually, upon applications (better food for the sick, allocations to enterprises).

Thus the market-clearing and regulatory function of equilibrium prices is replaced by state control, and we speak therefore of controlled prices and a controlled economy. But the latter has not been exhaustively described by what was said so far, because we have only dealt with control of a single branch of production and a single type of good. We have seen that relative market-clearing competitive prices establish also a balance of production and consumption among different goods, in the sense that labor and capital do not shift from producing one good to producing another. Competitive equilibrium prices automatically regulate also the allocation of labor and capital to the production of different goods. Their market-clearing and allocative (regulatory) function may also be replaced by state control. Indeed, it must be replaced because relative prices are no longer competitive prices automatically clearing the markets, but administered relative prices.

The state determines–from the solidarist viewpoint–whether there should be transfer of productive resources from one branch to another, e.g., from production of consumer goods to production of military goods. The impact will be felt within individual branches, e.g., as restriction of the number of enterprises producing for households and as rationing of goods (raw materials), of capital, and of labor (more will be said below).

There is still the question at what level will the state in the controlled economy set prices of different goods and thus also relative prices. Conceptually (legally) this could be any level, because once prices are set at levels other than equilibrium, the state must, in any case, use controls to replace the lost market-clearing and allocative (regulatory) functions.

Clearly, the further the prices are removed from equilibrium, the more compulsion is required to enforce them and the more controls—such as restrictions of consumption, etc.—must be used to replace them. However, from the legal standpoint, the intensity of compulsion is a function of the state's power to compel. After all, in pure solidarism some would perhaps be compelled to work for nothing, and what they produced might go to others who had perhaps contributed no labor or anything else. But things should not go that far. The government of the controlled economy wishes to retain the business enterprise system of production and therefore business enterprises as well. It only wants to change the automatic allocative (regulatory) function of prices, replacing it with its own purpose-oriented controls. But if it wishes to retain the entrepreneurial system of production in a controlled economy, it cannot fix prices at random, because this might destroy profitability, the motivating force of enterprise activity. If it destroyed business enterprise it would destroy the foundation of the controlled economy and it would have to adopt an alternative system of production. Consideration of enterprise profitability is decisive both for setting the prices of specific goods and for establishing relative prices of different goods (since the price of one good may be the cost of producing another).

A controlled economy on a capitalist foundation also starts out with capitalist prices that had been formed normally, prior to the onset of the abnormal conditions that led to the controlled economy. They were market-clearing prices and, as such, allowed certain production costs and made it possible for enterprises to operate profitably. Costs of production were proportional to prices, for otherwise the factors of production would have been moving toward production characterized by more favorable relationships of prices and costs. Prices and price ratios were not cost determined but, costs followed prices. But since the controlled economy does not need market-clearing prices to determine costs, it can use costs as the basis for price setting.

However, costs differ in any branch of production made up of a number of large and small enterprises operating under different conditions, even though, under competition, they sell their products at identical prices. Which cost is to be used as the basis for price setting? There is an ordered set of enterprises ranging from those operating at higher costs to those operating at lower costs. The former have lower profits, with which they are content, and thus manage to stay in business. If the decision makers of the controlled economy set prices on the basis of cost plus a percentage mark-up for profit, and if they choose the lowest production cost of the industry, they will reduce the profits of enterprises that operate at such low costs (and make the highest profits) but they will make continued operation impossible for enterprises that operate at higher costs. To the extent that low-cost enterprises can make up for the output of enterprises with higher costs, (and hence lower profitability—as is sometimes the case in manufacturing industry), the state may accelerate the process of rationalization (concentration of production in the most profitable enterprises) by setting prices on the basis of the lower production costs. In doing so, it may of course reduce the number of small and medium enterprises and hence the psychological support for the business enterprise system of production. Who would favor the enterprise system of production if there were few entrepreneurs? And there would not be many if the small and middle-size entrepreneurs disappeared. They would lose their independence and become employees of other enterprises. How far the state will go in drawing this critical line depends on its concern for business enterprise production in different industries.

And so the entire system of prices and price ratios is built upon a hierarchy of costs, selected administratively so as to rationalize production. Non-reproducible goods (works of art, antiques, unique products) necessarily remain outside this system, as do some enterprises about which more will be said below. We speak of a hierarchy of prices because, in the last analysis, the costs of all goods consist of the compensation of labor and capital (ultimately costs do not include prices of other goods, because the prices of such goods—primary raw materials—can again be broken down into compensation of labor and capital). And so the problem of prices in the controlled economy leads to the problem of labor and capital markets.

(b) The price of capital.

Under competition the price of capital balances the demand for and supply of capital funds and channels capital to those economic units that require investment funds from those that make them available (through savings, through liquidation of enterprises).

When the price of capital—the rate of interest—is displaced from its equilibrium level, both these functions are lost, and when the state controls the rate of interest it must replace them. On the supply side control will assume the form of forced saving, etc., to provide a sufficient volume of capital. On the demand side it will involve making certain that the most urgent projects are taken care of. Forced saving can be accomplished easily, particularly where incomes are paid at regular intervals, e.g., wages and salaries, on a monthly, weekly, or other regular basis. Here should also be included measures directed against hoarding, intended to actually bring capital funds into the money market. As for borrowing, this concerns particularly the question of assuring that the state's interest in new credits (war credits) is accommodated. If it is, there will be no need to float new loans in the money market because credits will be granted to the state directly by the financial intermediaries. It would be possible to set up priority rankings for private enterprises except that the circumstances that lead to the establishment of the controlled economy tend rather to a plethora in the money market.

The question is, at what level should the controlled economy set the rate of interest? If capital formation is controlled and enforced, there is no need for higher interest rates to stimulate the propensity to save. Lower interest rates imply then the possibility of raising the share of labor and a closer approach to the ideal of the "right to the undiminished proceeds of labor". Conceptually, if all economic activity were controlled and compulsory, this could lead to the abolition of interest. Of course, we would then have a purely cooperative or solidarist economy. After all, the existence of interest on capital means that enterprises pay attention to the factor of time in economizing, that capital is fully employed, etc. There is no capitalism without the rate of interest.

However, if the rate of interest were arbitrarily lowered below its equilibrium level, and approach zero, there would be serious consequences. We are not even concerned with various funded institutions such as the capitalized social insurance system, founctions, etc., which depend on interest income, and lose some of their substance whenever interest rates decline. (They could be bailed out by contributions and state assistance). We are rather concerned with the rate of interest being the basis of valuation of all rents, above all ground rent, and land itself. Prices of land are determined by capitalization of rents at the current interest rate. In a competitive market these prices would rise astronomically. Of course, the controlled economy would extend its regulatory powers to the price of land as well (rents in perpetuity). But, the cost principle is not applicable here. Price ceilings could be initially set on the basis of previously experienced competitive prices that were determined—among other factors—by competitive interest rates. However, if the rate of interest declined still more, prices would no longer correspond to rents capitalized at the lower interest rate. Many people would want to buy land and invest money in land, but no one would be willing to sell land at the controlled prices. Sales of land would come to a complete halt and it would become necessary to ration land at the administered prices which the land owners would correctly regard as confiscatory, because they would represent only a part of land value. Whoever got a piece of land would receive a free gift at the expense of the former owner. If the state wished to prevent disintegration of the capitalist system of production on this account, it would not arbitrarily lower the rate of interest.

(c) The labor market.

The problem of administering the labor market, so as to replace the lost market-clearing and regulatory functions of equilibrium wages, differs, depending on the direction of the displacement of the wage rate from equilibrium.

Under normal circumstances, the administration of the wage rate will tend to set it above the equilibrium level, so as to improve the condition of the workers. The consequence of such displacement will be unemployment, because many individuals will seek jobs at the high wage rates, but at such wage rates enterprises will be unable to employ all of them. Administration of the labor market would then mean compelling households and enterprises to employ more workers than they would find useful given the wage they would have to pay (e.g., an employer who would otherwise employ twenty workers would have to employ an additional one). Alternatively the state itself would have to assume the burden of caring for the unemployed, or else stimulate additional production to serve its purposes, and so make it possible for enterprises to create more employment without incurring losses.

However, under extraordinary war-time conditions, there may appear shortages of labor which will be in demand particularly by the state to produce military goods. Under competition the state would have to bid up wage rates and raise the price level, to be able to hire the necessary workers. Administered wage rates would then be set below equilibrium levels, and the state would have to compel workers to supply labor just as it compels grain growers to supply grain. It would have to impose on every able-bodied person the duty to work and allocate labor to different industries, according to their importance, just as it allocates goods (raw materials, etc.), in agreement with the solidarist systemic principle which replaces the lost allocative function of competitive prices.

The question is again whether the state could raise wage rates arbitrarily to improve the position of wage workers. In capitalism it is possible to improve the relative position of labor—given the level of national product—only at the expense of the share of capital and entrepreneurial profit. This is so because prices, which are not cost determined, form an all-inclusive framework that cannot be exceeded (provided that money is based on some good, e.g., gold). The matter is different in a controlled economy, even though it preserves the business enterprise system. Here, prices are determined by costs, and if costs are administratively raised then there is nothing in the way of prices being also administratively raised in proportion to the rise of wages, while preserving an unchanged percentage of enterprise profit and an undiminished compensation of capital. This corresponds to inflation in pure capitalism. Of course, this is not an improvement of the workers' position, except to the extent that existing money capital is devalued and capital's share in national income reduced. However, if the state wishes to maintain the purchasing power of money, it cannot increase the compensation of labor, since it would bring about the above result; on the contrary, it must disallow such increases.

But now we come to the most difficult task of the controlled economy: Wage rates for different kinds of labor must be set so that aggregate compensation of labor should equal the value of the national product that labor produces (less compensation of capital and enterprise profit), and so that wages for different kinds of labor should fit in this aggregate according their technical merit in contributing to the national product. To start with, the controlled economy takes over wages from capitalism, but their subsequent adjustment–if it is not to be entirely arbitrary–is just as difficult here as in national cooperation. Of course, the controlled economy may also introduce solidarist principles in the wage determination process (according to need, according to number of children, etc.), which would cause a loss of the connection and direct relationship between performance and reward, and would necessarily lead to compulsion to assure some level of performance, etc.

(d) The foreign exchange market.

The exchange rate establishes balance between payments to foreigners and payments from abroad, primarily payments for imports and exports (here we omit discussion of other payments; for details see my *Soustava národního hospodářství [System of National Economy]*, Vol. 1). We buy abroad, we import from foreign countries, we acquire goods that are less expensive abroad than at home, and we make payments to foreigners. Conversely, goods that are less expensive at home are exported, sold abroad, and payments are received for them. Whether foreign goods are less expensive depends also on the price of foreign currencies (of foreign exchange, e.g., of short-term notes denominated in foreign money). If one can obtain a Swiss franc for 3 crowns, everything becomes less expensive in Switzerland (including living there) than in our country. If one has to pay 20 crowns for a Swiss franc, everything in Switzerland becomes too expensive for us, when translated into our money. And so for each exchange rate there are some foreign goods that are cheaper for us, which are therefore imported, and for which payment is made to foreigners. Other goods are cheaper in our country, from the point of view of foreigners. These are therefore bought from us, and payment for them is made to us. A fall of the exchange rate causes an increased flow of goods from our country to foreign countries; a rise of the exchange rate reverses the flow. The exchange rate tends to settle at the point where payments to and from foreign countries are in balance.

The exchange rate could then fluctuate without limit, which would make it difficult for exporters and importers to make their calculations. The state wishes to stabilize the exchange rate of its currency relative to foreign currencies. This would come about automatically, if the currency was based on gold, and the central bank stood ready to sell unlimited amounts of gold for its bank notes. This result would occur because—if there was a deficit in the balance of trade—importers could buy gold for export from the central bank. Gold from the central bank would thus supplement exports of goods, to maintain equilibrium in the balance of payments. Conversely, if there was a surplus in the balance of trade, the central bank's holdings of gold would increase. However, no central bank could withstand a prolonged deficit in the balance of trade; its reserves would disappear and then there would be nothing to stop the exchange rate from falling (the value of foreign exchange would rise). The central bank would have to apply downward pressure on domestic prices (deflation) by decreasing the quantity of money and raising interest rates. In this way it would create a relationship between domestic and foreign prices that would be more favorable for exports, and conditions that would be less favorable for imports (foreign goods which were formerly cheaper would become more expensive). The exchange rate would be stabilized but, instead of a fluctuating exchange rate, the central bank's pressure would cause the general domestic price level to fall, leading to domestic recession and disturbances caused by falling prices.

To avoid this (given a large deficit in the balance of trade) the state turns to currency regulation, i.e., it sets the exchange rate at some level relative to foreign currencies and regulates payments to and from foreign countries. If the fixed exchange rate is above equilibrium relative to the balance of payments, and if the domestic price level is too high, relative to both (this would call for a policy of deflation), payments from abroad (i.e., exports) would tend to decline automatically, and would have to be artificially stimulated by export subsidies. Conversely, imports—which appear as very advantageous (foreign goods are less expensive)—would have to be restricted according to their importance (the solidarist principle). One could also levy import duties which could be used to finance the export subsidies. Balance of payments equilibrium is thus artifically maintained and so is a fixed exchange rate. The state can follow a policy of maintaining balance of payments equilibrium either vis-à-vis all foreign countries (so that a deficit with one is offset by a surplus with with another) or else vis-à-vis each country separately. This is especially facilitated by bilateral clearing arrangements between the central banks of each pair of countries, where payments going to a foreign country are offset by payments coming from that country. If there are no incoming payments, then the outgoing payments are held up. There is a deficit in the balance of payments and foreigners are granting us interest-free credit. Continuation of this credit (before it is offset) which is a function of the size of the balance of payments deficit, causes losses to exporters; the export prices that they realize are lower (if they do not get paid for a year, then their present price is lower by an amount corresponding to the domestic discount rate). Such "frozen" credits act as a brake on exports; the interest lost by the "freezing" has the same effect as if the country with a balance of payments deficit had a lower exchange rate.

The state need not concern itself–indeed it cannot concern itself–with flexibility of the relationship between the balance of payments and the domestic price level, because it sets the latter directively on the basis of the set of selected costs. The relationships among currencies, which is the basis of the clearing arrangement, may differ from country to country as need dictates.

8. Money in the controlled economy

When exchange and free choice of goods exist, so does money. We know however that the nature of money differs, depending on how prices are formed. Price is an expression of exchange of one good (money) for all goods (the set of all goods) because money, as such, is a claim on the set of all goods, in selected proportions. It is a good of indirect abstract usefulness. When one of the traded goods serves as money, prices can be calculated simply–if we know the exchange ratios between the money commodity and other goods. If the exchange ratio between meat and flour is 5 to 1, and if 1/2 kilo of flour is the unit of account, then the price of 1 kilo of meat is 10 units of money. Prices are merely a form of exchange ratios between goods. What is the basis of these exchange ratios? Two individuals will continue trading (we assume for simplicity that goods are divisible) as long as exchange adds to the utility of each, as long as a kilo of his trading partner's good (which he receives in trade) yields to the trading individual more relative utility than does his own good which he trades for it. Both individuals think in these terms, and they cease trading when they no longer have an incentive to do so. This occurs when the relative utility of the good received no longer exceeds the relative utility of the good given up, i.e., when the marginal relative utilities of each good are equal. Only considerations of utility (not of costs)* are relevant for exchange and exchange ratios, and hence for prices and for the value of money.

When there is a nominal money unit, with no connection to any physical good (in practice this means gold)–i.e., when there is a paper currency–then the exchange relationship of the money commodity (gold) exercises no restraint on the price level. E.g., if wages were administratively raised to more than enterprises could afford to pay at existing prices, they would raise prices. If the minimum legal wage rate was raised to 200 crowns per day, this would mean a crisis for the enterprises and would lead to unemployment. This could be resolved either by allowing prices to rise or by returning to a lower wage rate. Political pressure would follow the path of least resistance, management of the currency would take a back seat, and the problem would end up in inflation. With higher economic magnitudes** there would be a relative decline of the real content (purchasing power) of the legally fixed wage rate. In addition to the crisis of domestic production, there would also be a crisis of exports, unless the exchange rate fell.

The desire for monetary stability in capitalism, and the fact that the currencies of the economically most powerful nations are based on gold, has led to the fact that even nominal currencies are indirectly based on gold, to the extent that they are stabilized relative to gold-based currencies. This is how matters stand in capitalism. In contrast to this, prices in national cooperation, are formed on the basis of cost of production, in practice labor cost alone. The latter becomes directly the price and is therefore the sole price-determining factor. The unit of account is therefore a unit of labor, and its exchange value depends on the set of all goods that can be purchased with it.

The situation is similar in the controlled economy. Depending on the type of production cost that is selected, prices are administratively fixed

---

* Considerations of cost are relevant in determining the volume of goods produced, because production will not continue if cost exceeds the utility of the output. For details see my *Soustava národního hospodářství [System of National Economy]*. Vol. 1, 1938.

** See Translator's note pp. 45-50.

on the basis of costs. These are not simply labor costs, as in national cooperation, because here there is still entrepreneurial profit and income from capital, but they are mostly labor costs. The unit of account is only an abstraction based on prices that are set in this manner. It is not based on free exchange ratios but on fixed prices based on production costs. Hence the unit of account need not be one of the goods (some amount of gold). It need not conform to the external exchange rate of the currency (the price of the means of foreign payments), since the balance of payments too can be managed without regard to competitive forces. Indeed, there may be a different exchange rate for each foreign country (for clearing purposes). Money in the controlled economy resembles more closely money in national cooperation than money in capitalism.

Finally, currency management may also be controlled in the sense that money serves not only as medium of current payments but as money capital to finance investment. If such management is to be non-inflationary, the increased use of resources by borrowers must be accompanied by decreased use of resources (lower level of consumption) either voluntary or forced, elsewhere in the economy. The resulting savings (capital formation) must compensate the outlays made by management of the currency in the money market.

9. The organs of the controlled economy

The capitalist economy is guided by three types of domestic equilibrium prices and one foreign equilibrium price in four markets (goods, labor, capital, and foreign exchange).

The controlled economy takes over the market-clearing and regulatory functions of the markets and equilibrium prices. It follows that organs of the controlled economy—through which the state exercises these functions—correspond to those markets. The Supreme Price Office is a counterpart of the goods market, the Labor Office is a counterpart of the labor market, the Central Monetary Authority corresponds to the money market, and the Central Foreign Exchange Authority to the foreign exchange market. There may also be—above all these—a Supreme Authority which performs regulatory (solidarist) functions for the economy as a whole, paying attention to inter-relationships of all four markets.

Because what is involved is not merely the promulgation of general decrees but also adoption of measures that affect separate enterprises, these agencies cannot deal with the staggering number of all kinds of scattered enterprises. Instead they undertake to organize enterprises of the same type into associations that resemble cartels but perform different functions. Even existing cartels may become organs of the controlled economy, but their function changes. Their task becomes the implementation of the objectives of the controlled economy and the implementation–among their members and within their industrial branch–of what they are directed to do. Henceforth they become representatives and organs of the idea of the controlled economy, rather than representatives of the vested interests of their members. Membership in these associations–which can be organized hierarchically (separate branch associations within an overall industry association)–then becomes compulsory and binding. Employees are similarly organized in trade unions and trade union associations. In this manner is facilitated the enormously difficult administrative task which the controlled economy involves. Hence the associations cannot be granted autonomy, which they could use to successfully implement only the interests of their associated enterprices, but instead they are administered authoritatively.

10. A critique of the controlled economy

We must distinguish criticism of the essence of the controlled economy from its specific content, such as war-time controls, because the shortcomings of such controls need not be present in every controlled economy.

The essence of the controlled economy is the business enterprise system of production where equilibrium is determined neither by the competitive market nor by agreements of private economic units, but in a planned fashion, in response to prices (in the broad sense) authoritatively fixed by the state. The constitutents of equilibrium (in all four markets) are not brought into balance mechanically (e.g., so that production would match consumption), but according to the state's solidarist valuation (e.g., consumption is regulated according to need). Consequently, what is involved is a certain mixture of capitalism and solidarism. On the other hand, one probably cannot characterize the system as cooperative,* because it abolishes neither business enterprises nor profits (though they may be reduced to "management on a commission basis") nor interest. However, the admixture of solidarism in the controlled economy does not implement the "right to a living", nor does it tend toward an egalitarian distribution of income and wealth. It merely prevents such undeserved gains as would arise in an emergency situation where prices would be left to regulate the allocation of consumption, labor, and capital, because prices would then rise excessively to maintain equilibrium. Of course, at the same time, rising prices would also stimulate rapid expansion of production and capital formation. Not only are shortages prevented from harming the poor but limited supplies are allocated according to importance.

So far we have considered only intervention that lowers price when production is insufficient. But what if prices were low and there was overproduction? Would restrictions be imposed on production and prices raised as is done by cartels? This too is possible in the controlled economy. In sum, we can state the following about the controlled economy in its present-day form:

1. It is a system which has its origins in war-time emergency (or in preparation for war). In such an emergency it is the only possible and reasonable system, as evidenced by the fact that it is introduced by every belligerent nation. Controls must be maintained after the war as long as production is low and there are shortages of goods and capital (war production ceases).

2. Any displacement of prices from competitive equilibrium levels must lead to declining productivity (which is also true when prices are raised by cartels). The farther the fixed prices are from free-market equilibrium, the more unfavorable is the effect upon productivity. Consequently, if the state wishes to overcome post-war shortages it must gradually adjust prices in the direction they would tend to move if the market mechanism were in operation. Otherwise, it would have to use state funds to subsidize

---

* To be sure, national cooperation also involves a controlled economy, but that is a different kind of control than what we have in mind here when we speak of "the controlled economy."

production (e.g., in our country, in an earlier period, the state had to subsidize housing construction). A system which is in conflict with productivity cannot be a permanent program.

3. Controls are responsible for the economy losing its flexibility. The sensitive relationship of prices and production, of relative prices that guide allocation of resources to produce different goods, of prices–in the broad sense–and the corresponding markets (prices of goods, interest rates, wage rates, exchange rates) and of capital movements between markets (balance-of-payments deficits are deflationary, balance-of-payments surpluses are inflationary, etc.)–all these relationships and reactions, which tend to automatically remove distortions are lost and replaced by authoritative fiat which is not even capable to fully grasp everything and to be flexible with respect to adaptation and change. The system becomes rigid.

4. The controlled economy brings about a special kind of unfreedom. The producer and the consumer face each other. The consumer has his income and he would like to buy more goods at the given prices; indeed he would gladly pay more to get more goods. The producer has an opportunity to sell but he is not allowed to take advantage of it. Everyone is thus constantly tempted to break the law. The black market accompanies every controlled economy like a shadow, and not even the threat of the most cruel penalties is of any help.

5. Control of the labor market takes away the original function of trade unions and, just as it forces producers to make deliveries, it compels workers to perform compulsory and unfree labor. The relationship of employers and employees becomes troubled and strained, since it is no longer based on mutual interest but on compulsion. Workers' and employers' freedom no longer exists. That too is bound to have unfavorable effects on performance and productivity. The state must set the wage level and relative wage rates of different kinds of labor–a difficult task also faced by the cooperative economy.

6. Entrepreneurial profit is an "engine" which powers the activity of the entire national economic "machine". If controlled prices are not profitable in this sense, then the activity stagnates, and when it does it cannot recover. Controls are a defense against overproduction and unemployment, against distortions originating abroad. This applies in particular to an exporting country.

7. If the policy of a controlled economy were a permanent policy it would exclude political democracy because the tasks of the state could not be dealt with by majority vote of the participants. This would lead to an authoritarian regime or, at least, to extraordinary powers of democratic governments. Of course, this is not inevitable if the controlled economy lasts only a limited time–e.g., during a war and during a post-war period when a start is made to re-establish continuity with pre-war relationships.

8. The state administrative apparatus faces an extremely complex task requiring a vast bureaucratic apparatus staffed with experts, and involving correspondingly huge costs. Both state administration and business enterprises experience proliferation of activity associated with "controlling". Bureaucratic work expands relative to manual work.

This critique of the controlled economy applies only to an economy which in other respects remains a private capitalist system. We must not confuse it with the "control" implemented by the state in national cooperation or solidarism. Obviously, the economies of these two systems also require state control, but this is, of course, an altogether different "control" (planning) from that with which our critique is concerned.

XII. TRANSFORMATION OF THE CAPITALIST SYSTEM

The profit motive, which is essential for capitalist entrepreneurship, motivates enterprises to strive to increase profitability by excluding free competition among themselves. Enterprises in a given industry (producing similar products) engage in price competition for sales and for customers, until price settles at a point where production and consumption are in balance. At that price it does not pay an enterprise to produce more than is demanded by consumers. If enterprises, in their drive for larger profits, reach an agreement to charge a higher price, that price can be maintained, provided they do not underbid each other. But at the higher price there will not be sufficient demand to sell as much output as at the lower price.

These organizations (cartels, syndicates) may be formed among competitors on either side of the market. If they are to survive they must take steps to change the level of output of their member enterprises to restore balance between reduced consumption resulting from higher prices, and production, which must be accordingly restricted as well (quotas, re-allocations). Cartels cannot raise prices arbitrarily. They can raise them—beyond a certain point—only at the expense of profitability of their member enterprises. Profit per unit of output would increase, but the number of units sold would decrease, in such a way that total profit would be smaller than with a lower price and larger sales. Consequently there exists, at some price, a maximum profit of the cartel members, and this is a natural limit of price increases by the cartel. All this was already noted above.

The cartel price is very different from the competitive price. Although it is market-clearing, it is not an outcome of competition between entrepreneurs and consumers. Instead it is established unilaterally and perpetuated by a cartel of enterprises* which dictates the price and thereby indirectly determines the volume of consumption to which production is adjusted in a planned way. The market order of production and consumption in a given branch of industry, its relations with other branches, and hence its connections with markets for labor, capital and foreign exchange, no longer arises spontaneously from competitive interplay of all interests in the economy, but in an arbitrary and planned fashion.

If competitive prices perform a regulatory function, not only with respect to the balance of production and consumption, but also with respect to income, competitiveness vis-à-vis foreign countries, and the balance of payments, then the effect of cartellization of even one branch of production must lead to distortions of the general competitive equilibrium order.

What is most important is that cartel prices are higher (or lower) than competitive equilibrium prices, and this implies that production corresponding to these prices is no longer at a maximum. In seeking maximum profitability**, productivity declines. However, the main advantage of competitive capitalism is the fact that competition generates an automatic equilibrium order and leads to maximum productivity. Productivity and economic progress are the main advantages of the capitalist system. In other respects capitalism offers many reasons for social criticism. And now there arises, from the womb of the system, from its most salient element, from its motive force, an organization which undermines the system's fundamental advantages.

---

* Alternatively, price may be determined by agreements of associations of cartels.

** In what follows we refer only to cartels of business enterprises.

Suppose that all branches of production become cartellized, and that the producers of a good face—as buyers—the producers of all other goods. Though they had raised the price of their product, their higher money return would not help, because, in turn, they would buy all other goods at higher prices. In the end they would merely succeed in lowering productivity. The system would have lost its fundamental characteristic advantages.

Faced with this development, the state could not remain indifferent in view of the public interest. For this reason it has viewed the development of cartels, from the very beginning, with ambivalence. At first it refused to extend legal protection to cartel agreements, declaring them to be without legal power. But the cartels did not require legal protection since they possessed sufficient means to enforce their discipline upon entrepreneurs. At one time the state did ban both producers' cartels and workers' syndicates, but eventually, in accordance with the policy of liberalism, these prohibitions went overboard. Besides, they could not stand in the way of natural development. Subsequently the state placed no obstacles in the way of efforts by trade unions to raise wages but was chiefly concerned with the harmful character of producers' cartels and their tendency to raise prices. It began to deny them tariff protection, thus inviting foreign competition when domestic competition disappeared. The cartels responded by organizing internationally. Eventually the state gave some thought to state price fixing and price arbitrage tribunals, but this also failed to be effective, in view of the heterogeneity of production costs in different enterprises.

Meanwhile cartels evolved, from their beginnings when they simply tended to raise prices and restrict production, into organizations with important other objectives. In the first place, they tended to achieve internal rationalization of production. If production was to be restricted, the restriction would take primarily the form of closing down enterprises operating least advantageously, at highest costs. These enterprises had to be compensated from contributions made by other enterprises, and cartels thus also became financial economic centers of the associated enterprises. Similarly some cartels came to face further tasks. If a particular industry depends, to a large degree, on exports and price competition abroad, it needs to be compensated by higher prices of its domestic sales. And if it is economically rational that enterprises located close to the country's borders, on waterways, etc., should produce for export, one could not impose on some the losses from exports and grant to others the gains from domestic sales. It was natural that cartels became centers for financial equalization among enterprises. E.g., in our country this was the case with sugar. If the state decides to subsidize exports, the cartels are a ready-made economic center for distributing subsidies designed to maximize the volume of exports. The state may also use this center as agency for collecting consumption (turnover) taxes or for refunding business taxes.

All these phenomena indicate that cartels evolve into production centers, to which the enterprises of a given industrial branch become completely subordinated. Cartels are transformed into higher economic units which determine the aggregate level of production, and possibly the elements of costs. They generate the total return, re-distribute it, etc. Thus far development along these lines has not been the same in all industrial branches; it has been easier particularly in those industries whose product is simple and typical, e.g., sugar, alcohol, etc. But this development shows the way. The state can achieve through the cartel, what it desires and what is in the public interest, provided that it does not merely stand on the outside, as law giver, promulgating directives and prohibitions, but joins the cartel as direct participant and shareholder, sharing in its revenues and guarding the public interest, though leaving its administration to private management and private initiative, in the interest of economic efficiency, and serving the public interest through effective control of the cartel which has now become a public body. There is no reason why workers and other employees should not participate in management as co-entrepreneurs and why they should not receive their share of profit directly from such center.* Private management (even if the state held the majority of the capital shares) would free the state from the burden of efficiently managing.

In addition the state would have to create, from among its representatives in individual cartels, an umbrella organization that would perform functions that had formerly been performed by the competitive market as regards relative prices of goods and as regards the relations of markets for goods, labor, capital, and foreign exchange. Rationalization carried out in entire branches of industry could bring about great economies.

---

* At one time, after World War I, I suggested this for coal miners in my proposal to socialize the coal mines.

And we shall have to rationalize, because of the great shortage of capital that we shall experience after the war (an excess of currency in circulation is not an excess of capital). We shall be therefore forced to economize capital, and if capital is not to be allocated by rising interest rates, we will have to manage and regulate its uses in the most rational way. Priority must surely be given to reconstruction of productive facilities that provide earnings and employment rather than consumers' comfort. And if production requires financing it is important, from the viewpoint of the economy, that rationalized production receives the financing.

And so it seems to us that in the new postwar [Czechoslovak] economy cartels may have a new task to perform. The controlled economy has already turned them into its organs and endowed them with a public function. Just as development in different industries has differed because of the different nature of their production and products, so the task of cartels will not be the same in the postwar economy. It is reasonable to build on the foundation of what was created through natural development, if one can achieve in this way all that any economy necessarily desires,–maintaining and improving productivity, rationalizing production and labor, sustaining social progress, as well as public control of all that. It is clear as day that the internal structure of that higher economic unit will change, particularly as regards the independence and continued existence of the lower economic units, the individual enterprises, within the framework of the higher unit.*

---

* This suggestion, written during the war, was overtaken in our country by nationalization of industry and the start of the road to national cooperation.

XIII. ECONOMIC SYSTEMS AND INTERNATIONAL TRADE

In capitalism the volume and structure of production are ultimately determined either directly or indirectly, by subjective valuation which guides the purchases of individuals (consumers). This determines individual prices which guide profit-seeking enterprises in producing consumer goods and capital goods. Goods are produced in quantities that consumers perfer and are able to buy with their incomes. The volume and structure of imports are determined analogously, since consumers do not usually inquire in the market (store), whether a good is produced at home or imported. They buy goods in accordance with their subjective valuation. In this way they determine prices and thus motivate enterprises either to produce goods at home or to import them. We can therefore say that how much of what is imported depends ultimately on subjective valuation of domestic consumers. The volume and composition of imports is not guided by some objective need of the nation, as supplement to domestic production required to maintain the nation's life, health and culture, not by objective utility, by its importance. Instead it is guided by subjective valuation alone. What is imported is what people want and what they are willing to buy (and pay for). Accordingly, imports are not centrally administered. They are not under state control; they are engaged by profit-seeking enterprises.

Exports depend on utility valuation of goods by foreigners. This leads to prices that the foreigners are willing to pay, while domestically the profit motivation of enterprises determines whether it is more advantageous to sell abroad than at home. Balance of exports and imports in the framework of balance-of-payments equilibrium is accomplished by the price mechanism whose description is beyond the scope of this essay. (See my *Soustava národního hospodářství [System of National Economy]*, 1938.) However, changing prices (of domestic outputs and of imports) cause changes of relative utilities of goods, and hence of the volume and structure of purchases.

From the viewpoint of the nation as a whole we may say, even in capitalism, that exports are a means to pay for imports, because through imports the nation obtains goods at less expense, more economically, than by producing them directly; alternatively it obtains goods that it would not otherwise produce at all. Thus the Czechs "produce" cotton or oranges in their crystal glass factories and by exporting sugar they use their land to get more and cheaper wheat than they could by direct production. Of course, in capitalism no one thinks of all this when exporting. This economizing is not directed from some center, by a plan; it arises spontaneously. Exporters do not regard exports as a means to pay for imports, but as a money-making activity which promises a larger return than domestic sales. The price system enforces economizing.

The capitalist state may intervene in foreign trade to maintain balance of payments equilibrium, to protect domestic production, and even to regulate consumption (imports may be harmful to health or morals), through various controls, such as tariffs, which affect prices and relative utilities, quotas and embargoes on certain imports and exports, and by subjecting exports, imports, and allocations of foreign exchange to its approval. The state's actions are mostly negative, because initiative remains with individuals and their valuations. What is more or less important as regards state prohibitions, approvals, etc., depends again on valuation, but here it is valuation based on the ideal of the nation's life, health, and culture, i.e., state solidarist valuation. Here begins a combination of capitalism and solidarism.

In capitalism comparison of foreign and domestic prices plays an important role where exports and imports are concerned. However, since the prices that are being compared are expressed in different currencies, an international market in currencies and means of foreign payments (foreign exchange) also emerges. What is bought are not only foreign physical goods but foreign currencies (i.e., foreign abstract goods). too. When buying money one buys power to purchase and power to make payments regardless of where that power comes from, i.e., whether money represents a concrete good (gold) for which it is exchangeable, or whether it is fiat money. A paper currency too has an exchange rate. However, one always buys a currency that can be used to purchase anything abroad and import it (money that can be used to make payments abroad). The foreign exchange market presumes the existence of a goods market. It is important to realize this because in solidarism, for example, there is no domestic goods market.

What is the nature of foreign economic relations (exports and imports) in national cooperation? Here all goods are brought to the market by the state, because the state controls all production and sells it in its stores. The state is therefore the only exporter of a part of its output, using the proceeds to buy imports. There are no profit-seeking enterprises that would produce for export or undertake imports. Again we assume a state with a purely cooperative economy.

The task of the cooperative state is to serve the subjective wants of its citizens, and if the citizens demand goods that can only be obtained abroad, in exchange for other goods produced at home, foreign trade will take place. But the cooperative state also faces the task of serving the subjective wants of its citizens most economically i.e., of obtaining goods for them at the least labor cost. There is no other cost in the cooperative state, because the cost of material inputs represents in turn the cost of labor which produced these inputs. Hence, there emerges some labor-cost ratio between good A and good B, which is the basis of prices in state stores (relative prices). Let us say that the ratio is 1 to 2; if the exchange ratio that prevails in the world market is one unit of A for one unit of B, it is more economical not to produce B at home but to produce A for export and trade each unit of A for one unit of B, i.e., at half the cost.

Here, because there is only one buyer of foreign goods and only one seller of domestic goods, there is no need for domestic money in the international market. The state makes use of foreign money both to buy and to sell. Its own currency is not traded in foreign markets.

If all foreign trade in national cooperation is concentrated in state hands, the state will naturally also pay attention to solidarist considerations, particularly with respect to imports, and import only goods that are most important from the viewpoint of the solidarist objective. Therefore it will not import what the citizens subjectively prefer merely because it can be obtained cheaper from abroad (as it would in pure national cooperation) but only what is objectively most useful for them and for the collective, assuming of course efficient utilization of labor.

What is the situation in pure solidarism? Here the state does not really ascertain, and hence does not know, production costs expressed either in money or in labor (technical) units, because it assigns labor according to capacity to work, i.e., to those for whom it means relatively smallest loss of life, health and culture. Production costs are precisely these losses, which differ among individuals performing identical work. A purely solidarist state is actually a vast self-sufficient economy, comparable to a family that produces all that it requires and consumes what it produces, allocating labor according to capacity to work and goods according to objective need. If such family decided to trade with an outside economy, it would do so, in the first instance, only on the basis of utility considerations; it would trade a good yielding relatively less utility for one yielding relatively more utility up to the point of equality of relative utilities. But subsequently it too would organize production to take advantage of exchange opportunities, if it were possible to obtain a good more economically by trade than by direct production. But imports are always valued by the state in accordance with objective (solidarist) importance, while exports are only the means to obtain important imports.

The solidarist state does not have money (endowed with indirect abstract usefulness); there are only vouchers for some goods. Hence there can be no foreign exchange market (if for no other reason than because individuals are not permitted to acquire foreign exchange—only the state can). The state buys abroad and sells to foreign buyers for foreign currencies; it also projects its own relative utilities—when it values imports and exports—in terms of foreign currencies. Foreigners do not acquire the currency of the solidarist state, since such currency does not exist (it cannot be used to make purchases) and even if it did exist, they would be unable to use it freely to make purchases in the solidarist state.

It can be seen that a country's exports and imports are the outcome of valuation that corresponds to its economic system. A country which has gone from capitalism to solidarism will have a very different structure and volume of imports than it had before the transition. This must be taken into account by exporting countries. A country that exports luxuries and urgently requires foreign raw materials, will be unable to keep up its exports, if the states which were its customers undergo a transition from capitalism to solidarism. Such country would rather be interested in free world trade.

If economic cooperation of two nations and countries is understood to mean trade among them, then consideration of such cooperation cannot ignore their economic systems, because the latter determines the volume and composition of exports as well as export techniques (monetary and payments aspects) and export policies. In capitalist countries foreigners may encourage exports by influencing consumers and their psychology (through advertising). This is not possible in a solidarist country or a national-cooperative country with solidarist control of foreign trade.

The controlled economy maintains equilibrium of the balance of payments artifically and it must therefore control one side of the balance of payments, the one that tends to cause disequilibrium. Alternatively, it may control both sides by artifically strengthening the weaker side (exports) through export subsidies. Imports can either be restricted mechanically, maintaining equilibrium through the clearing method of payments, or else through the import-approval procedure. The clearing method allows foreign trade to flow freely according to subjective valuation, but imports are paid for by exports (if there is a clearing balance). If there is no clearing balance, then the importer waits and loses interest—which implies that the price (to the foreign exporter) is lower, as if the exchange rate of the importing country fell—until imports cease.

But the import-approval procedure requires valuation of the importance of imports, and this is only possible from the viewpoint of the solidarist purpose just as it is with respect to allocation of goods and capital in the controlled economy.

XIV. THE FORMAL-POLITICAL STRUCTURE AND THE MATERIAL FUNCTION OF THE STATE

1. Introduction

Every collective (society, church, corporation, municipality, the state, etc.) endowed with legal personality must have a rule specifying how that collective formulates the single will that is its will as a legal person. This rule is its *constitution.* It specifies how the organs that act on its behalf are established and how their continuity is maintained. Their actions are considered from the normative viewpoint–whether they are in agreement with the constitution, whether they are carried out correctly, according to the constitution, and whether they are therefore valid. The constitution may establish different organs for different expressions of will–for example, a legislative assembly, a cabinet, courts of justice. It may also establish different conditions for the validity of such expressions of will. Every collective possesses such constitution, organs, and forms of expression of will (a society has its general meeting, executive, president, secretary, etc.; a municipality has its municipal council, executive committee, mayor, and possibly also a general meeting of its citizens; a corporation has its shareholders' meeting, board of directors, supervisory board, chairman of the board; the state has its legislative assembly, which promulgates legal norms, courts of justice that make judicial decisions, cabinet which issues administrative acts, etc.). The constitution may state the principle according to which the representative will is formulated—either by a simple or qualified majority. All this represents the *formal structure* of the state (or some other collective). In the case of the state we speak of its formal-political structure.

Even if we knew (from its constitution) all about the formal-political structure of the state (or some other collective) we would know nothing of the content of its will, of its activity. Two societies with identical formal structures may have the most varied *activity contents,* to which we shall refer as their *material functions,* i.e., purposes which they strive to achieve. The constitutions of non-state collectives (organizations, legal persons) must also specify their material functions, their fields of activity (delimit the content of their will), though only in general terms. The content of the objective that delimits their material function constitutes their task as seen from the normative viewpoint (e.g., care for youth of a certain kind, education, assistance to poor members of a society, etc.). Conceptually, the constitution of the state need not include such delimitation of its material activity. From the legal viewpoint, it would be sufficient to have a constitutional statement about its formal-political structure, because, from the purely legal standpoint, the only question that must be decided is the question of the validity of norms promulgated by the state organs. To determine this, it is sufficient to consider constitutional provisions that indicate who can promulgate valid state norms, and in what form they must be promulgated. There is no need for additional provisions concerning the order which the state proposes to keep for its citizens (because that is its material function). And if there were no provision concerning this matter, the state could keep or change any order, with a given constitution containing only provisions about the state's formal-political structure.

However, if the constitution also contains—in addition to provisions about its formal-political structure (which is the rule)—provisions about its material function, then we must carefully distinguish these two aspects, not only because they are teleologically and legally distinct, but also because there exists a certain relationship between these two aspects, which is discussed in this chapter. The relationship is that of appropriateness or inappropriateness (adequacy or inadequacy). However, we must first consider the basic distinctions between possible types (systems) of both aspects.

2. Systems of the formal-political structure of the state

In principle only two systems are possible: The nation (the people of a state) is either the *agent* of state power, or else only an object of that power. Accordingly, we distinguish systems of *autonomy* (democracy) and *heteronomy* (authoritarian system, dictatorship).

If the nation is to be autonomous it must be ruled by a single will formulated by the nation as a whole. The nation is not autonomous, if it is subject to outside will, either the will of another nation, or the will of one (or more) of its members, but independent of the will of the collective. The central will must be formulated by the nation electing (on the basis of the principle of majority) a central representative body (legislative assembly, cabinet) which then represents its will, but which is always dependent on that will–assuming that periodic elections take place. The nation formulates the central will out of the will of all individuals who are free to make decisions (elections), who must know what choices there are with respect to issues and persons, and who must be therefore endowed with freedom of conviction and its expression (freedom of the press) and freedom of association. In all these respects, they must be protected by courts of justice which are independent of the government. Autonomy of the nation presumes autonomy of the individual. As far as details are concerned, there may exist different forms of democracy, but the essential feature is the autonomy of the individual. Its significance is that everyone is free to inquire what is good and what is better, so that the nation cannot permanently stray.

The opposite of democracy is heteronomy, an authoritative system (dictatorship). Here the will of the ruler stands opposed to the will of the nation which is merely the object of government independent of its will. There can be also transitional forms between these two systems (e.g., constitutional monarchy). Even a dictatorship may be good for a nation, if it pursues the purpose of the nation's objective welfare and also avoids demagogy (lying to the public, making false promises to gain its favor). a more detailed exposition is beyond the scope of this essay.

3. Systems of the material function of the state

This refers to the economic and cultural order that the state establishes for its citizens. We have considered its types in the above discussion of economic systems which include:

I. Individualistic systems:

   a. the free market system,

   b. the system of national cooperation;

II. The solidarist system.

The systems were described and their mutual relationships were discussed above, and the reader may refer to what was said there.

4. The mutual relationship of the formal-political structure and the material function of the state

It is understandable that the substantive content of government depends on who governs, and that a certain type of government can be expected only from a certain type of ruler. Consequently, there exists—between the formal structure and the material function of every collective (organization)—a relationship of appropriateness (adequacy) or inappropriateness (inadequacy). We shall demonstrate this on the example of a joint stock company. Its formal structure consists of the shareholders' meeting, the board of directors, the supervisory board, and majority decisions of stock holdings at the shareholders' meeting. Its material function is to make money for the capitalist shareholders (through production, trade, etc.). Suppose that we change this formal structure so that each shareholder gets one vote at the shareholders' meeting, regardless of how many shares he holds. The result would be that the meeting would also distribute the corporation's profits on this basis, not on the basis of the number of shares owned. A single share held by a shareholder would give him a hundred times higher dividend than a share held by a shareholder with one hundred shares. Such inequality of dividends would make trade in the stock impossible, it would cause disintegration of large share holdings, and the corporation would collapse. Such formal structure is therefore inadequate for the corporation's material function and vice versa.

And so it is also with respect to different formal structures and material functions of the state. It does not follow from the concept of a government how it shall govern, nor does it follow from the concept of a material function what type of government it requires. The question is not one of logic since a logical relationship is not involved. A particular relationship of the formal-political structure and the material function of the state comes to light only when we make a specific assumption about the psychological make-up of the citizens—that they are, in our experience, egoists. The relationship would change immediately if we assumed that they were perfect altruists.

Experience teaches that we can, indeed must, make the empirical assumption that all men are more or less egoistic, that if their behavior is to be contrary to their egoism, they must be compelled to it, and that behavior under compulsion is never as effective as when the agent is motivated by self-interest. On the basis of this empirically based assumption we shall now examine the question of what formal-political structure is appropriate or adequate for various systems of economic and cultural order among men (the material function of the state).

The citizens regard the state in two opposing ways: the individualistic and the solidarist viewpoint. In the first case they see it as an organization that serves their interests as citizens. The state is therefore seen as a kind of cooperative organization for maintaining order and providing external defense. There is therefore nothing in the way of the state will being formed democratically from the will of all individuals (by elections, government of the people for the people).

A state that implements a solidarist order stands opposed—as agent of will—to the nation, which becomes the object of state care directed toward the ideal of life, health, and culture. Here the nation (the people) cannot be the agent of government. The government cannot be based on and depend on the will of the people, because the people, who are egoists, do not want a government that forces them to self-sacrifice. Such state cannot therefore start out from the interests of the citizens (what they subjectively desire). Here one should carefully distinguish the two meanings of the word "interest", which may refer either to the objective or the subjective welfare of the individual for whom something is done. He may be subjectively opposed to an objective utility (e.g., taking medicine may be unpleasant; it is not in his *subjective* interest, though it is in his *objective* interest; it represents an objective, not a subjective utility).

In addition to this solidarism involves objective welfare (interest) of the nation as a whole, to which the welfare of the individual–not only subjective but often also objective welfare–is subordinated. Given the egoism of men, one cannot expect that they will support a government that implements solidarism. Solidarism demands heteronomy, not autonomy of the nation. The central will of the state stands opposed to the nation as a whole. This is precisely what a solidarist state is.

Individualism includes two distinct systems, the free market system and (pure) national cooperation. However, the state which controls all production in national cooperation, faces the problem of distribution (there are no unearned incomes, no interest, no rent, no enterprise profit). Generally speaking, the principle that only labor and labor merit should form the basis for compensation and distribution of national product, can be easily implemented by elimination of business enterprise through nationalization of industry, and abolition of the labor market and of private ownership of the means of production (e.g., land). However, the question how to distribute the national product among various individuals according to the various kinds of work that they perform cannot be solved on the basis of some general principle of merit. Merit is either subjective (effort) which cannot serve as an objective criterion, or else objective (output). In a free market economy the value of a good does not depend on the labor devoted to its production, and cannot therefore serve as measure of labor compensation. However, in national cooperation the value of the product is a function of the quantity of labor devoted to its production, so that the value of labor cannot be derived from the value of the product but vice versa. There is no objective labor unit that could be used as a measure of the value of each type of labor (various types of industrial, agricultural, intellectual, etc., labor).

In a free exchange economy labor compensation is determined by equilibrium in the labor market, by agreement between businessmen and employees and their unions, as an outcome of struggle. This is not so in national cooperation where wages are decided by state decree. Labor unions do not have the right to strike, because this would mean conflict with the state and its decrees and would be tantamount to insurrection (sabotage). But what then is to be the basis for the norms that set out different wages and salaries (the state wage tarrif)? Are they to be established by vote of the workers employed in an establishment or vote of workers in all establishments? The outcome of such vote would tend toward equalization of wages and salaries, because there are more below-average and average than above-average workers. However, equalization of wages and salaries would also mean equalization of performance (above-average performance would disappear) and thus a decline of national product and the nation's living standard. If such an unfortunate outcome of a "democratically" established wage schedule is to be avoided, the wage schedule must be decreed heteronomously (authoritatively). The state cannot permit public discussion of this matter. Discussion of the wage schedule (and everything connected with in) by the press or in public assemblies cannot be allowed. This economic and cultural order leads therefore to an authoritarian political system because of the impossibility of discovering a labor unit to serve as measure of the compensation of labor and of the degrees of that compensation. We shall not pursue further the question of what considerations the state should take into account in establishing labor norms and labor compensation because it is only a question of discovering the relationship between the particular material function of the national-cooperative state and its formal-political structure.

The democratic political structure is thus compatible only with a state whose material function is the free market. The free market system requires that the state have a democratic structure which, in turn, makes the free-market system possible. Consequently, those who demand democracy as the formal-political structure of the state in politicis demand eo ipso the system of free markets—though perhaps limited—as the material function of the state in oeconomicis.

5. Systems of formal structure and material function of the state and the "natural rights of man"

Every social order implies duties for some and—the converse—rights for others. Every right presumes someone's duty, and both presume an order from which they follow. Every social order can be therefore focused on the individual and his rights. We speak of "natural" rights, but there are no rights that derive from nature, only from particular social orders (we do not speak of "natural" duties). And why should not animals also be endowed with natural rights? Instead we have recently begun to speak of "human rights".

In outlining those human rights it becomes apparent that they follow from the democratic political system (personal freedom, freedom of conscience, freedom of belief, and their expression in free speech, free press, freedom of assembly and association, and protection of these freedoms—even against the government—by an independent judiciary). But even the material orders of the state can be and are sometimes projected as individual rights. Thus the right to work and the right to undiminished proceeds of labor correspond to national cooperation and the right to a living corresponds to solidarism. A dictatorship, of course, grants no rights to individual citizens. Accordingly, we can formulate the following schema:

A. Formal-political structure of the state

I. Democracy (autonomy)

Human rights: freedom of conscience, of thought, of religion, of elections, of the press, of assembly, and their protection by an independent judiciary

II. Heteronomy (dictatorship)

Human rights do not exist

B. Material function of the state

I. a) the free market system

Human rights: to engage in money-making activitiy, to trade, consumption, private ownership of all goods

b) national cooperation

Human rights: right to work, right to undiminished proceeds of labor, private ownership of consumer goods

II. Solidarist system

Human rights: right to a living, no private control of goods

It follows that socialism, which would include both national cooperation and solidarism if it were fully realized, would not permit democracy as the political form of the state. If human rights are declared to be only democratic political rights, this means that, in principle, they are compatible only with the free market system.

The same idea about the adequacy of the formal-political structure of the state for its material function can be also applied to intra-state organs and supra-state bodies. An organ whose function is to carry out the will of the government cannot be properly selected by election and be responsible to electors. It cannot receive directives from above and, at the same time, be responsible to electors below—unless its responsibility to the electors is only apparent and its members can be recalled by order from above. Judiciary organs whose activities are supposed to be guided only by considerations of normative justice, cannot be properly appointed by the choice of political parties which pursue different goals that their members must follow. Otherwise they would be guided by their partisan tasks in performing their judiciary function. They would not think only normatively but—depending on the goals of their party—also teleologically, and therefore not in accordance with objective justice. A supra-state organization that would attempt to subordinate its member states in a solidarist way would generate centrifugal forces that would subvert its cohesiveness. For example, a provincial body that would rely on voluntary cooperation of delegates representing various regions (regional bodies) would not get much cooperation because of the resistance of the more affluent regions which would have to subsidize the others.

And so when a body (organ) is to be set up one should always pay attention to the adequacy of its political structure for its material function, and vice-versa. Otherwise they may obstruct each other and even tend to bring about a process of disintegration.

XV. THE "PLANNED" ECONOMY AS A PROGRAM OF SOCIALISM

1. Introduction

We have noted that all socialist factions share a negative attitude toward free market capitalism, but that their criticism and the postulates derived from it run along two lines. It can be said that all socialist factions propose nationalization (of goods, of the economy) but that state ownership is not a program, because it is compatible, as such, with different, mutually contradictory economic orders (of production and consumption of goods, of allocation of goods and labor) namely national cooperation and solidarism.

Following the two World Wars that brought the controlled economy where—it appeared—prices could be lowered and wages raised to any level, the socialists came to view the state-controlled economy with favor. It seemed desirable to extend controls to the entire economy and it seemed that this would solve all the major social problems—even without nationalization. Socialists therefore started to call for a "planned economy", i.e., an economy controlled by state plan, as opposed to the unplanned free-market economy plagued by the major evil of unemployment. This new slogan came to be a program common to various shades of socialism—a positive program, as against the negative attitude toward the free-market system, which they shared and against the conflicting postulates of solidarism and national cooperation. Both of these lead to state planning of the entire economy, and it is therefore claimed that the state can abolish all unemployment arising from overproduction that characterizes the unplanned system of free markets. However, planning is not the same in the two systems. It is therefore necessary to consider first the essence and the differences of planning, and then show what form it takes in different economic systems.

To plan an economy, to budget, means to draw up a set of balances of all outlays and receipts (sources and uses of resources) perhaps including also physical balances that underlie the budget figures. A uniform plan can only be applied to a uniform economy, with a uniform objective. For example, one cannot draw up a common plan for both a consuming economic unit (household) and a producing economic unit, just as one cannot keep common accounts for them. Suppose that a cobbler kept a single set of accounts for his business and his household: E.g., so many crowns for hides; so many for his wife's dress; so many for glue; so many for flour, etc. And suppose that he would sum up all these items, or use them as the basis for drawing up a budget. How could he compare one item with another as more or less important? And that is precisely what must be done when planning the economy. After all, the economy employs resources (money) in accordance with relative utilities, and these utilities—if they are to be comparable—must be homogeneous. Subjective utilities of households cannot be compared with objective utilities of business enterprises (incremental returns). And utility is homogeneous only when it follows from the purpose that is common to a given economy.

This error was also implicit in the state budget, of Austria-Hungary, which was drawn up uniformly along ministerial lines, so that expenditures of the State Railways and the State Tobacco Monopoly were added together with expenditures on Social Care and Welfare. The former were expenditures of state enterprises, while the latter were solidarist outlays (household expenditures by the state financed by transfers of taxes). We know that the state sector is by no means homogeneous, that is a complex consisting of a homogeneous solidarist economy, state cooperative establishments, and state business enterprises. Treating such expenditures jointly and adding them together is the same error as above in the case of the cobbler. It means adding magnitudes that cannot be mutually evaluated and therefore rationally planned. It is most important to realize this, in order to consider state planning in various economic systems. Common budgeting for heterogeneous economic units is nonsensical; it is a contradiction of planning which involves valuation of what is more or less important.

Planning (budgeting) is the outcome of valuation by the economy's decision maker. His valuation either depends only on his considerations or on consideration of the valuation of other individuals and other economic units as well. In the latter case, he can only estimate the economic magnitude of the various items; he cannot determine the actual expenditure beforehand. For instance, if the state tobacco monopoly plans sales of tobacco, and different kinds of tobacco, and accordingly plans the purchases of raw materials, it does so on the basis of expectations of sales of tobacco products based on previous experience. But if tobacco sales turn out to be different, e.g., if they rise—because of changing subjective valuations of smokers—the state will, in turn, increase its raw material purchases. Hence figures for sales of the product and purchases of raw materials are only non-binding estimates. But this is also true for any business enterprise that plans its purchases or, similarly, for any cooperative that serves for other economic units. On the other hand, the volume of net investment (as distinct from replacement investment) of the state tobacco monopoly (additional equipment) does not directly and immediately depend on buyers of tobacco products. It depends only on valuation by the state as agent of the tobacco monopoly enterprise. The plan figures for such investments can be binding, at least as maximum figures (because even here, where the state makes decisions based only on its valuation—just as in the solidarist sector of its economy—it must take into account, in a money-using economy, price changes and natural physical changes (harvest, etc.). With this qualification we can draw a fundamental distinction between a non-binding plan or budget, which is merely an estimate or program that can change, depending on the will of the agents of the economic units, and a plan or budget which is binding for the economy in the course of the economic planning period. If various aspects of activities of business enterprises and cooperatives were rigidly fixed, it would have to lead–in consequence–to disturbances of their operations and of the interactions of economic units (enterprises).

And now we can investigate economic planning in different economic systems.

2. Planning in the free market (capitalist) system

This system is sometimes described as unplanned, but this is only true to the extent that not all economic activity is guided and planned from a state center, because the economy is not monolithic. Nevertheless, each business enterprise, each producing economic unit, draws up a program for the forthcoming period, a plan which is not binding, since enterprise activity also depends–among other things–on its customers. Consuming economic units (households) also have their plans of purchases, according to relative utilities, which are carried out in the customary way, within the budget constraint. Purchases change not only as a result of changes in consumers' subjective valuation, but also as a result of price changes, because they are made according to relative utilities. Consumption increases when a good becomes cheaper; it declines when it becomes more expensive. However, it is impossible for all production and consumption to be centrally planned because there is no central control and the economy is not monolithic. (We consider the state sector separately.) The only regulators of all economic activity are free-market prices which balance production and consumption and are set by competitive forces. To each price corresponds a particular quantity consumed (purchases are made according to relative utilities) and a particular volume of production (production is carried on according to relative costs, according to what is more profitable). Each business enterprise and household pays attention to the prices which guide their behavior. When there is no equilibrium, prices rise or fall to restore balance of production and consumption. However, this is only a market-clearing system, not one that ranks the nation's production according to importance. Production choices originate with buyers (consuming economic units) and are therefore made on the basis of subjective valuation by innumerable consuming units which find such production appropriate. Production continuously adjusts to them, seeking to maximize business profits.

Those who seek in planning a weapon against unemployment, blame the "unplanned nature" of the free-market for disturbances of production, for lack of correspondence between production and consumption, for over-production, and hence for unemployment. Business enterprises adjust to fluctuating demand for different goods imperfectly, as evidenced by major economic depressions. However, one may also ask whether inflexible state intervention which erects a rigid framework for private business activity is not also responsible for the persistent duration of depressions, by making speedy adjustment more difficult.

By insisting on a fixed relation of its monetary unit to gold, the state prevents rapid restoration of balance of payments equilibrium, in much the same way as it would prevent ending an overproduction crisis by fixing product prices at high levels that would prevent restoration between balance of production and consumption. Fixing wage rates in long-term wage-schedule agreements may also impose a rigid framework upon a living organism. Similarly, any other intervention from a position of power reduces the system's ability to adjust.

If one seeks in planning an alternate organization of producing goods than that which prevails in the free-market economy, whose range of production and consumption reflects the subjective valuations of consuming economic centers, this implies that state planning involves other objectives.

The free-market system is found nowhere in its pure form. In addition to a large amount of regulatory legislation which intervenes in free production, consumption and exchange, there exist numerous public economic bodies (municipalities, districts, provinces, the state) which are an organizationally alien element. They are not monolithic economies with uniform purposive orders. They are complexes of several different economic systems. We shall, therefore, deal with the planning (budgeting) of these public economic bodies, after we have examined planning in all economic systems.

3. Planning in the system of national cooperation

In national cooperation the role of consuming economic units (households) is the same as in free-market capitalism and what was already said about their planning in the free-market system also holds. However, here one must also consider aggregate consumption of each good, because this is decisive for planning the corresponding production. Statistical data on consumption in a prior year may serve as basis for estimating consumption in a subsequent year. Of course, that part of planned production that corresponds to this can only be a program, rather than a binding plan, because consumption depends on subjective valuations–based on relative utility–of consuming centers (households) whose demand motivates production. What this implies can be estimated on the basis of past experience, but cannot be determined in a binding way. In planning production in nationalized industry (provided that its volume depends on human will–cf. agriculture!), the state may therefore formulate nonbinding production programs for individual producing establishments. But if such plan were declared legally binding, it would become rigid, and production based on it would confront consumption that fluctuates and changes in accordance with subjective valuations of the consuming units. It would lead to overproduction in some branches and underproduction in others until such time as productive resources were re-allocated from the branches with surpluses to those with shortages.

If one is concerned with the percent of plan fulfillment rather than the percent of satisfaction of consumption demand, then it appears that planning involves binding directives. It could then not be regarded as success if the plan, that matched a correct estimate of consumption, was overfulfilled. To exceed the plan would actually mean over-production and failure to fulfill it would mean that consumption was not adequately supplied. Consumption is understood here to include the demand of productive establishments, supplied by other cooperative establishments with raw materials, auxiliary substances and semi-finished products.

There remains the problem of measuring output, relative to the plan, as aggregate for individual establishments producing different products or groups and complexes of such establishments. Consider the simplest possible case of a single establishment producing three goods: *a, b,* and *c,* in different quantities (regardless of whether this is or is not in accordance with the plan). Suppose that 60% of production time is devoted to producing *a,* 30% to *b,* and 100% to *c*. Suppose further that this results in an output of 100 units of *a,* 50 units of *b,* and 20 units of *c*. However, let the plan be 125 units of *a*, 75 units of *b*, and 5 units of *c*. The plan for *a* is therefore under-fulfilled by one-fifth (20%), in the case of *b* there is a shortfall of one-third (33.3%), and the plan for *c* is overfulfilled by 300% (the excess of output is three times the planned output). For a single homogeneous product (e.g., iron rods) one can easily calculate by how much (units or percent) the plan was overfulfilled or what percent of the plan was attained. But how can one make such calculation for a whole establishment? The simplest (but also least correct) method would be to add the percentages of plan fulfillment of the different goods and take their mean. In the above case it would be 80% in the case of good *a* (out of the planned 125 units the achieved production was only 100 units), 66.6% in the case of good *b* (actual output was 50 units compared to the 75 units that the plan called for), and 400% in the case of good *c* (actual output was four times larger than planned output). The sum of these percentages is 80 + 66.6 + 400 = 546.6, and the mean is 182.2%. This would imply that in the aggregate, the establishment overfulfilled the production plan by 82.2%, i.e., that output was more than four-fifths larger than planned, which might be viewed as a great production success. And yet, everyone knows that this is not so.

The same error is involved here as if we measured the purchasing power of money or–which is the same thing–the cost of living, by a single number (an index number) derived by taking for each good (e.g., meat, bread, pepper) an equal unit of mass (e.g., one kilogram) and then considering its price at two different points of time, and thus obtained the average price of a basket of goods–and conversely, the purchasing power of money–disregarding the fact that households buy incomparably larger quantities of meat and bread than pepper. Suppose that the price of meat and bread fell by 20% (from 10 to 8 in the case of meat and from 5 to 4 in the case of bread) but that the price of pepper rose by 200% (from 50 to 150); three units of these goods formerly cost 10 + 5 + 50 = 65 and now cost 8 + 4 + 150 = 162; the sum rose by 97, i.e., by almost 150 percent, although it is apparent that the cost of living did not rise, when we take into consideration the quantities of meat, bread, and pepper which the households buy in the aggregate. When prices change one cannot assign equal importance to each good but an importance in accordance with total consumption. Such mean is called a weighted mean and it is the only correct measure.

Let us now return to the increase or decrease, as the case may be, of production in a multi-product establishment. The percent increase or decrease of output of a single good does not consider the importance and volume of its output within the framework of production of the establishment as a whole. Therefore, the mean of such percentages is totally useless and leads to erroneous conclusions. Once again, it would have to be a weighted mean, which would pay attention to these factors. But how does one derive a weighted mean? In measuring changes in the cost of living, one can consider the quantity of each good purchased as part of aggregate consumption. By the same token, the importance of the output of different products of an establishment would have to be commensurable in terms of some common unit. Could this be mass or some other physical unit? If a farm were to change its production plan and substitute potatoes for a previous output of industrial crops (hops, poppies, etc.), it would experience a considerable increase in the mass of its output. Could it be said then that its output has increased as a result?

The importance of the output of different goods in a free-market enterprise was naturally given by its price in the framework of the aggregate output of the enterprise (all products) since the enterprise is, after all, interested in making money and the money unit is the common measure of the exchange value of all goods. Of course, prices are determined here by market forces, not directly by production costs and labor costs. On the contrary, here the equilibrium price sets a limit to economically feasible production costs, including labor costs.

However, in national cooperation there are no markets and hence no equilibrium prices that would set the limits of production. In a free-market economy, consuming units make purchases according to relative utility, and producing units produce according to relative costs. But, in pure national cooperation, prices are determined by the compensation of labor for such production. The former is decided by the state in the production plan, and the latter by labor-input norms. All goods thus involve labor costs, and the importance of different goods in the product mix of an establishment or of the economy could be weighted in accordance with them. Unfortunately, there is no labor unit with which we could measure the amount of labor embodies in different goods, to be able to say, for example, that good *a* contains 20 and good *b* 40 labor units and accordingly to value the aggregate output of *a* and *b* of an establishment (or the national product). If there is no technical labor unit, there is no compensation unit for labor. (If there were one, it would be the unit of account of the national cooperative economy.) Hence the compensation of labor is decided arbitrarily and authoritatively. Nevertheless, compensation of labor is the only thing that can be used to measure the importance ("weight") of the output of individual products with respect to each other and within the overall product mix of an establishment or in the national product, though it is not a correct unit (it is a labor cost); but there is no other.

We face an analogous problem when we wish to determine what increase (or decrease) of output has taken place in a multi-product establishment for which the cost of production (compensation of labor) has been accepted as common denominator in the framework of total output. We wish to arrive at a single number describing the increase or decrease of output in an establishment on the basis of the volume of production of different goods. These magnitudes must be homogeneous. One cannot obtain a single figure showing an increase or decrease of output or an average from the mass of one good and the number (pieces) of another. Hence, we search again for what all products have in common and what can express the increase or decrease in which we are interested. Indeed, this holds even for the same type of good of different quality and quantity. If an establishment produces coal and from it tar, coal oil, etc., how can we express by a single figure the increase or decrease of its production?

In a free-market economy we would again use prices to express the value of aggregate output on the basis of the production prices of individual goods. In national cooperation there is no market (equilibrium) price, there is only labor cost which was already used to express the significance of the output of particular goods within the framework of an establishment's total production. In the free-market economy changing prices express changing demands in the economic environment of the market. But, this assumes constancy of the value of the money unit in the two periods, when measurement is undertaken. If the national product of France were in the trillions of francs it would be no larger than when it was in the hundreds of billions of francs—if the value of the franc had meanwhile fallen as a result of inflation. In national cooperation there exists not even this tool to measure the growth or decline of aggregate production of different goods. The only thing that there is, is again labor cost.

In the free-market economy the monetary unit is a good—either one of the goods (gold) or—in the case of nominal currency—a conceptual set of goods representing a miniature living standard. Therefore we measure production, and its growth or decrease, again by means of a good. Its value is of course not perfectly constant. It may change because of state action (inflation, deflation). But in the national cooperative economy, labor cost is not the total price, because a mark-up for investment and state administration is added. It is only the resulting higher price which then regulates consumption and which is relevant for expressing the purchasing power of the money unit and the cost of living. However, this price cannot very well measure the volume of output. Furthermore, if wage rates were based on time (time wages) it might appear that production was unchanged, when the same number of hours had been worked, when in fact labor productivity declined.

Similar difficulties as those encountered in measuring the volume of output are also encountered when attempting to express, in aggregate terms, the degree of plan fulfillment. So far we have discussed fulfillment of the plan of consumer goods purchased by households, to which should be added replacement of machines used to produce these goods because this represents a portion of their production costs. However, the national cooperative economy produces not only these goods. There is also net investment. How and on what basis is the decision about net investment made?

Net investment is undertaken in a free-market economy by business enterprises, if they expect that it will result in profitable production, i.e., production yielding a return that exceeds the interest on loans used to finance it. Enterprise investment decisions are therefore made in accordance with equilibrium in the money market and the interest rate. None of this exists in national cooperation because there are no business enterprises and there is no money market. There exists therefore neither an incentive for nor a limit to investment. If the state in the national cooperative economy nevertheless undertakes investment, then it no longer acts as a cooperative state, interested only in "the undiminished proceeds of labor" but as a solidarist state endeavoring to improve living standards either by reducing the burden of labor with unchanged output or by raising output with an unchanged burden of labor, in order that the nation may progress toward its ideal of life, health, and culture. The incentive to invest is to be found in the pursuit of this ideal. And in pursuing it the state acts independently of any other economic unit and its valuation; it decides on the basis of its own valuation. Hence, the plan of such investment is not just a program, but a binding plan. And what is the nature of the valuation that we attribute to the state? Investment projects employ a segment of the labor force which is thus unavailable for the production of consumer goods, does not make a living by producing them, and must be maintained by the rest of the population. This happens in such a way that the income of the rest of the population is reduced either directly, by reducing wages, or indirectly, by raising prices of consumer goods. For example, if a third of the labor force is employed on investment projects, wages of the rest must be reduced by one-third, and the amount by which their wages are reduced must be paid as wages to those employed in producing investment goods. The same would be achieved if the one-third was raised by imposing a 50 percent tax on the price of consumer goods since everyone would then be able to buy a third less with the same income. It is possible of course to use a combination of these two methods. Hence maintaining the producers of investment goods implies that the rest of the population must bear a sacrifice by means of which is obtained a lighter burden of labor or a higher living standard in the future. The sacrifice takes the form of reduced current consumption and it could also take the form of additional labor. How much the population can be compelled to sacrifice for the sake of future benefits in one of these ways is a matter of solidarist valuation. It depends on the state, and the investment plan can therefore be a binding plan.

The economic plan of producing consumer goods in national cooperation is only a non-binding program; the plan of net investment results from solidarist valuation, and can therefore be a binding plan.

4. Planning in the solidarist system

Money—which still exists in national cooperation—does not exist in solidarism and hence the economic plan cannot be expressed in money terms but only in physical terms, as a listing of physical goods. Also, the solidarist economy is a single, monolithic economy ordered according to relative costs (capacity to bear sacrifices) and relative utilities (needs) whereas the cooperative economy is a complex of productive establishments whose objectives are technical (to produce a given output with minimum labor cost). In national cooperation the volume of production of individual goods is not an outcome of valuation of what is objectively needed, but an outcome of the demand of consuming economic units (households) based on their subjective valuation. The one and only decisive factor in solidarism is objective state valuation based on the ideal of life, health, and culture, independent of the subjective valuation of individual citizens. The state plan can therefore be binding (with the qualifications noted above about the effects of nature, etc.). If the plan is binding with respect to consumer goods and replacement investment, it is so a fortiori with respect to production of investment goods. The solidarist state can draw up a single plan for the entire economy, but of course only in physical terms. The plan cannot be aggregated because output cannot be expressed as a single figure there being no single unit of measurement.

5. Planning of the state's own economy

We know that the state sector in the free-market economy is not monolithic, that it is a complex of several systems which includes a solidarist core (financed out of the budget) a number of cooperative productive establishments (financed by charges paid for their services), and a number of state enterprises (financed from the proceeds of their market sales). For its sector the state draws up a budget that must be subdivided according to its composition. It formulates no plan for the private sector (private business enterprises, households). They formulate their own plans.

The question of planning arises in the case of national cooperation and solidarism. In solidarism there are no longer any private economic units, there is only a monolithic solidarist economy free of either cooperative or private-enterprise elements (of course, we have in mind pure solidarism).

And what of the situation in national cooperation? Here all production is carried on by the state. But not all economizing, because alongside the nationalized production sector there are free consuming economic units, each with its own "plan". Private business enterprise has disappeared and state cooperative establishments (formerly financed from charges) have merged with the national cooperative sector in a single set of cooperative establishments.

In addition to this, is there also a separate state sector? Indeed there is because in any case there is a solidarist core of the state economy financed by taxation based on ability to pay. This solidarist core is a complete and genuine economy, quite distinct from national cooperation and which cannot be integrated in the revenues and expenditures of the cooperative economy. In any case, it must have its separate plan, which is binding, in contrast to the plans of cooperative productive establishments which are non-binding and are only programs.

The separate budgetary items of the solidarist core can be valued—individually and in the aggretate—as more or less important from the viewpoint of the ideal of a nation's life, health and culture. This cannot be done for individual cooperative establishments (either individually or in the aggregate), because outlays of each are determined separately by buyers without regard to other establishments. Cooperative establishments do not compete with each other but within the solidarist sector an outlay can only take place when all the requirements of the sector and the overall capacity to make sacrifices are taken into account. The state therefore requires—even in the cooperative economy—a program of expenditures for cooperative productive establishments as well as a binding plan for the solidarist sector, which must also include the mixed cooperative sector that is financed in part by taxation.

6. Planning as a program of socialism

The proposal to plan is formal because planning can be undertaken in any economic system, and the proposal says nothing about the order which the plan is supposed to create, and which forms the plan's content. Even if planning is understood to mean state planning there is still a fundamental difference between planning of the purely solidarist sector and planning of the state-guided cooperative economy. In addition to the distinctness of the two social orders, the distinction between the two kinds of planning concerns also the point whether planning can be binding or whether it can only be a program. This is so because planning of the solidarist economy can be binding, whereas in national cooperation the planning of current production can only be a program, and only investment planning, which is based on solidarist valuation, can be binding. But, since there is no other (consistent) socialism, in addition to national cooperation and solidarism, it follows that planning does not represent a homogeneous concrete socialist program.

The state plans the entire national economy either in national cooperation or in solidarism, that is, in economic systems other than capitalism (which the socialists oppose). In calling for a planned economy, they certainly oppose capitalism and they certainly demand a system different from capitalism. But that is about all, since planning is fundamentally and thoroughly different in national cooperation and in solidarism.

In national cooperation the state can draw up only an estimate, a program, but not a binding plan with respect to production for current consumption and replacement investment because production is carried on for the sake of consumption, freely chosen and subjectively decided by the citizens whom it serves. Hence the plan cannot be binding, because a binding plan would require that consumption should also be planned and controlled in a binding way. Accordingly, the plan of all the establishments producing consumer goods would also have to be binding, and any overfulfillment of the plan would necessarily have distorting effects on the entire economy, just as underfulfillment would.

Only the plan of net investment—as distinct from replacement investment—could be binding, since it depends solely on valuation by the state of how much it wants—or is able to—reduce the citizens' current consumption, or how much it can increase the burden of their labor, i.e., what part of the population can be maintained by the rest, in order to be employed in net investment projects. But these are not considerations that concern the cooperative economy, which serves only the consumption of the citizens. They are a proper concern only of the solidarist economy where attention is paid to the collective's capacity to bear sacrifices.

In the solidarist system where the entire national economy is state controlled and depends on state valuation, the state—as economizer—must formulate a binding comprehensive plan, both for production and consumption.

XVI. INTERNATIONAL SOLIDARISM?

By international solidarism we understand solidarism among nations analogous to solidarism among individuals as described earlier. The strong and the weak pool their resources for mutual assistance, to provide for evenly balanced development of all. In the latter case strong and weak individuals joined together; in the former case nations are involved. The weak call for solidarism because of self-interest since for them it means assistance from the strong; but the self-interest of the strong must be overcome. Solidarism among individuals first appears as egoism of the weak who point to the fact that the strong have surpluses while they themselves suffer deprivation and poverty. This constant complaint gradually develops into the solidarist ethic and eventually its implementation by the state.

Until now the same self-interest—perhaps even a stronger one—has prevailed among nations. We would expect the weak, or relatively poor nations to call for international solidarism and the formation of a corresponding principle of international justice. The relationships of nations are thus also individualistic and there is a corresponding ethic (embodied in international law). It is noted that some nations are endowed with vast natural resources, that they control raw materials, etc., while others only can acquire them by trade, by labor (by exporting labor). When this is perceived as unjust, this inequality of ownership motivates criticism analogous to the criticism of the wealth of the well-to-do by the poor whose self-interest had led to national solidarism, after the initial developmental stage of self-reliance has passed. Another criticism that follows the same line of argument calls for economical utilization of natural wealth on a world-wide scale. It considers it uneconomical when a nation controls vast natural wealth that it cannot use or does not know how to use. What is meant by such "lack of economy" becomes clear only when it is added that there are other nations that need the wealth and know how to use it. The criticism leads indirectly to the demand that natural resources should be used by those nations that need them most and know how to make use of them.

However we are still a long way from international solidarism. At first there were, among individuals, only capitalist relationships and capitalist institutions corresponding to exchange, built on exchange, and promoting exchange. Associations of individuals were at first cooperative. As time went on these cooperative associations became agents of solidarist care. As far as nations are concerned, thus far the only relationships among them have been, in this sense, capitalist, based on international trade. As yet there have been virtually no associations or bodies corresponding to cooperation among individuals. To the extent that we hear reports about efforts to provide monetary and credit assistance once the war is over, this would be the first cooperative bodies of this kind because assistance by economically strong countries is—as far as we know—never without its price, never altruistic, but based on the consideration that "such assistance serves one's own economy".*

---

* This was written during World War II. International *economic* organizations such as the International Monetary Fund and the International Bank for Reconstruction and Development, and the international *political* organization (United Nations Organization, UNO) are cooperative in nature. The UN is an analogue of the legal state that came after autocracy.

The individualistic ethic and the individualistic order among individuals bring about an environment where everyone can exercise care for himself without being disturbed and where the strong do not infringe upon the weak. From there the road leads to the solidarist ethic and the solidarist order where the individual no longer exercises care for himself and is no longer responsible for his welfare, but society as a whole (the nation) exercises care for itself—and thus for the individual too—through assistance of the strong to the weak. As yet an analogue, even of the first step, has not yet been fully attained among the nations; and the second step is a long way off.

Still, what led to cooperation among individuals and to solidarism (always partial) within the national community, was the awareness and knowledge that this was the only possible way to a secure and full life of the individual. It is for this reason that national solidarism is on the upswing. This development depends of course on progress of technology, of the economy, and of culture, because it is only at a certain stage of economic and technological development that social responsibility for the welfare of individuals becomes possible. An analogous awareness among nations, awareness of the importance of the family of nations, has barely seen the dawn (UNRRA). Perhaps the development of this awareness too depends on economic and technological progress that we cannot as yet foresee and that lies ahead of us.

XVII. CONCLUSION: BETWEEN INDIVIDUALISM AND SOLIDARISM

The present exposition of economic systems does not include an economic criticism, i.e., an evaluation based on the question how these orders affect labor efficiency, productivity, and comparative welfare.* We have been concerned only with an exposition of the ideational elements from which the various systems arise and evolve. Of course, in doing that it turned out that the ideational origin of both national cooperation and solidarism is a certain criticism of capitalism, but that this criticism is not economic but ethical, or—as it is also put—social (though we do not wish to define these concepts). By the same token we have abstained from criticizing national cooperation and solidarism from this point of view. Besides, such criticism would only be historical, not immanent, which means that a positive or negative economic valuation would follow from the essence of a system, because each has particular economic effects

* We have only presented an economic evaluation of the controlled economy which is not a separte economic system.

only when the moral nature of men and their mentality are given. If men were perfect altruists, even solidarism—which does not take into consideration labor merit in distributing output—would lead to great economic growth. We have abstained from such criticism because we do not wish to give the impression that we either recommend a particular system or warn against it. We are concerned only with pure understanding.

We have seen that utility and value, economic morality and the law are polarized between two opposites characterized, on one hand, by what man desires, what gives him pleasure, and makes him subjectively satisfied and happy and, on the other hand, by what is good for him, what enhances his life, health, education, etc., in short, what makes him objectively better.

Accordingly, utility and value are either subjective or objective. Utility—and therefore value (degree of utility)—is subjective when it expresses the ability of objects and events to serve man's subjective ends, his subjective satisfaction, freedom from worry, etc. Utility, and the corresponding value, is objective when it expresses the ability of objects and events to implement the objective purpose of care whose object is man and the nation, the ideal of life, health, and culture. Subjective utility makes man happier, objective utility makes him better. The polarity is expressed here by the contrast of subjectivism and objectivism.

A nation's economic order may be based on the principle that everyone is responsible for his own welfare, and everything is therefore based on subjective utility (and of course cost) and individual responsibility, which leads to an individualistic economic order. Alternatively, it may be based on the principle that the whole nation is the object of state care, and everything is based on the purpose of that care, the ideal of life, health, and culture, on objective utility that follows from that, and on social responsibility. This is the solidarist order. The contrast here is between individualism and solidarism. As we know, the individualistic order also includes national cooperation.

Certain ethical norms specifying how men should behave in a given order are derived from these orders. These norms are thus also polarized according to the contrasting purposes served by the individualistic and the solidarist orders. They either serve the purpose that all, including the weak, should pursue without disturbance by the strong, their goals in life, seeking satisfaction. This implies a negative ethic: Thou shalt not steal!, etc. Or else they serve the purpose of implementing, for the nation or for mankind, the ideal of life, health, and culture, which should be approached evenly by all (this implies a positive ethic: Love Thy neighbor, etc.). The solidarist ethic (sacrifice, love) stands opposed to the individualist ethic (virtue, justice, honesty).

To each system corresponds also a legal order expressing the principles of the above two ethics. The two legal orders are known as private law and public law. The distinction between them depends on the systemic purpose served by each set of norms (as postulates of the legislator).

All human endeavor moves between these two poles. It never tends consistently toward one pole, its valuation, its economic order, its ethic, and its legal system. It is always influenced by both. Sometimes it approaches one, another time it approaches the other—as if there was perpetual struggle between them. It is understandable that real-world orders are always a mixture of individualism and solidarism because individualism is an expression of the individual's will to live, his intuitive selfishness and his desire to be free. But it also presumes the life of the social collective, of the nation. Solidarism, on the other hand, is an expression of the will to life of the social collective, which completely subordinates the individual, but presumes his life. The correct path lies probably in a harmony of individualism and solidarism.

However, the degree of influence of each of these poles is conditioned historically. It depends on the psychic attitude of men (to what degree education overcomes selfishness in favor of a sense of community) and on the attained level of technology and social organization. Here may occur unexpected developments, and re-education of men may also bring some surprising results. But as long as the instinct of self-preservation remains the source of egoism, men will continue to be, to some degree, selfish, and therefore feel unfree in solidarism, because they will want something else than self-sacrifice for the collective. Man only feels that his freedom is not restricted by norms when he desires that which the norm does. This instinctive desire to be free will force some degree of individualism under any conditions.

In addition, man possesses an inherent desire for progress. This is brought about by competition, and presumes inequality and individual merit. Hence, it would be unwise to reject all individualism. But it will not even be necessary, if a certain level of technology and social organization will allow as much solidarism as is required to abolish all poverty and provide balanced development of the collective. Solidarism will then have the task of implementing a more even, and therefore lasting, development of the collective, and individualism will have the task of being the motive force of progress and welfare.

APPENDIX

SELECTED BIBLIOGRAPHY OF K. ENGLIŠ' WRITINGS

Books:

Apologia Finalitatis; rozprava o Tardym (*Apologia Finalitatis; Discussion of Tardy*) Praha, Knihovna sborníku věd právních a státních, 1946. Engliš here denies the validity of Tardy's suggestion that finality is reversed causality.

Finanční věda. Nástin theorie hospodářstí veřejných svazků (*Principles of Public Finance. Outline of Economic Theory of Public Corporations*) Praha, Borový, 1929. Also in German as *Finanzwissenschaft. Abriss einer Theorie der Wirtschaft der öffentlichen Verbände* Brünn-Prag Leipzig, R.H. Rohrer, 1931. Also translated into Spanish by Dr. Milič Kybal as *Karel Engliš' Introduction a la ciencia financiera* Coleccion Labor, Seccion X, Economia, no. 399-400, Barcelona, 1937.

Grundlagen des wirtschaftlichen Denkens Brünn, Rohrer-Verlag, 1925.

Handbuch der Nationalokonomie Brünn-Leipzig, Rohrer Verlag, 1927.

Hospodářské soustavy (*Economic Systems*) Praha, Všehrd, 1946.

Národní hospodářství. Příručka (*Economics Manual*), 2. vydání (Brno-Praha, Borový, 1929.

O poznávání a hodnocení. Rosprava se Zd. Neubaurem (*About Cognition and Valuation. Discussion with Zd. Neubauer*). Vyd. 1 Bratislava, Nakl. Právnickej fakulty slovenskej univerzity. V. gen. komisi V. Linhart, 1947.

Orízeném hospodárství (*About the Planned Economy*) Bráfova knižnice hospodářská sv. 1 Praha, Melantrich, 1953. In German as *Regulierte Wirtschaft* Praha, 1936.

Peníze (*Money*) Nakl. Úřednického peněžního ústavu v Brně, 1918.

Problémy hospodářské teleologie (*Problems of Teleology in Economics*) Sbírka spisů právn. a nár. hosp., sv. XLV Brno, 1930.

Teleologie jako forma vědeckého poznání (*Teleology as a Form of Epistemology*) Prague, F. Topič, 1930. German edition as *Begründung der Teleologie als Form des empirischen Erkennens* Brno, Rohrer-Verlag, *1930.*

Teorie hodnoty a hodnocení (*The Theory of Value and Valuation*) Praha, Melantrich, 1947.

Theorie státního hospodářství (*Theory of State Economy*) Praha, F. Topic, 1932.

Soustava národního hospodářství (*Systems of Economics*), sv. I & II Praha, Melantrich, A. S., 1938.

Vybrané kapitoly z národního hospodářství (*Selected Chapters from Economics*) Knihy pro každého, roč. III, sv. 3 Praha, Stání nakladatelství, 1925.

Základy hospodářského myšlení (*Fundamentals of Economic Analysis*) Sbírka spisů právnických a národohospodářských, sv. XI Brno, 1922. Also in German, published by Rohrer-Verlad, Brno, 1927; reviewed, for instance, by Professor R. Streller in *Zeitschrift fur die gesamte Staatwissenschaft,* Bd. 83 (1928), pp. 350 ff.

Articles:

"Bilimičovy námitky proti teleologická teorii hospodářské" ("Bilimič's Objections Against Teleological Theory of Economics"), *Obzor Národohospodářský*, 1932, pp. 585 ff. Also published in German as "Zum Problem der teleologischen Theorie der Wirtschaft," *Xeitschrift fur Nationalökonomie,* 1933, pp. 220 ff.

"Erkenntnistheoretische Kritik der Grundlehren Liefmann's," *Zeitschrift fur die gesamte Staatswissenschaft,* Bd. 88 (1930), pp. 240 ff.

"Erkenntnistheorie und Wirtschaftstheorie," *Jarhbücher fur Nationalökonomie und Statistik,* III. Folge, Bd. 77 (1930).

"Hospodářská hodnota" ("Economic Value"), *Obzor Národohospodářský*, 1927, II.

"Hospodářství a hodnota v Schackově hospodářské morfologii" ("Economics and Value in Schack's Economic Morphology"), *Obzor Národohhospodářský*, 1931, pp. 677 ff and 794 ff.

"Das Liefmann'sche Gesetz des Ausgleiches der Grenzertraege in der Konsumwirtschaft," *Jahrbücher fur Nationalökonomie und Statistik*, N.F., Bd. 109(1971), pp. 385 ff.

"Hospodářské zjevy jsou jednotné" ("Economic Phenomena are Uniform"), *obzor Národohospodářský*, 1927, I.

"Probleme des wirtschaftlichen Denkens," *Zeitschrift fur die gesamte Staatswissenschaft,* Bd. 84(1928), pp. 578 ff.

"Psychický a teleologický subjektivismus v cenové teorii" ("Pyschic and Teleological Subjectivism in the Theory of Price"), *Obzor Národohospodářský*, 1939, pp. 81 ff.

"Sociologicky důkaz o nemožnosti teleologického výkladu směny" (A Socialogical Proof of the Impossibility of Teleological Interpretation of Exchange"), *Obzor Národohospodářský*, 1932, pp. 441 & 531 ff. This is a somewhat misleading title of Engliš' answer to Maiwald's proposition that a teleological argument cannot apply to barter.

"Die wirtschaftliche Theorie des Geldes," *Archic fur Sozialwissenschaft und Sozialpolitik,* Bd. 47(1920), pp. 271 ff.

"Weddigenova sociologická teorie hospodářská" ("Weddigen's Sociological Theory of Economics"), *Obzor Národohospodářský*, 1929. See also "Weddigen's soziologische *Wirtschaftstheorie," Jahrbücher fur Nationalökonomie und Statistik,* III. Folge, Bd. 76(1929), pp. 161 ff.

"Užitek relativní a užitek mezní" ("Relative and Marginal Utility"), *Obzor Národohospodářský*, 1928, 405 ff. and 510 ff.

"Teleologická teorie hospodářská a normativní teorie právní ("Teleological Theory in Economics and a Normative of Law Theory"), *Obzor Národohospodářský*, 1929, I, II.

"Tschechoslowakei," in *Die Wirtschaftstheorie der Gegenwart,* eds. H. Mayer, F.A. Fetter and Rich. Reisch, 4 vols. Volume One: *Gesamtbild der Forschung in den einzelnen Ländern. Friedrich Wieser, In Memoriam* (Wien, J. Springer, 1927), pp. 193 ff.

ADDENDUM
to
SELECTED BIBLIOGRAPHY

The preceding "Selected Bibliography" appeared originally in *The Czechoslovak Contribution to World Culture*. Miloslav Rechcígl, Jr. Ed., The Hague, Mouton & Co., 1964, 340-341. It had a restricted scope being oriented toward the most important works of Karel Engliš. In view of the present, far more enlarged presentation of his thought, it was considered appropriate to enlarge the bibliography as well. However, the Addendum is still not an exhaustive list of all of Engliš' studies, reviews and papers.

The Addendum is based chiefly on material made available by docent Ladislav A. Fuerst of Prague, executor of Engliš' literary heritage.

All entries, whether referring to books or articles, are arranged alphabetically, except where the entry refers to a translated publication. In that case the translated title appears under the alphabetic listing of the original. However, if the original publication was already listed in the above "Selected Bibliography," then the entry is not repeated and the translated publication is entered separately under its own alphabetical classification, followed with a reference to the original.

It was also thought practical to quote a few opinions about some K. Engliš' books. They are listed in the concluding section of this Addendum.

Chudinství v království českém na počátku XX. století. The Poor-Relief Laws in the Kingdom of Bohemia at the Beginning of the XXth Century. Monograph. Prague, Zemský statistický úřad, 1908; XIII. Also in German as *Das Armwesen im Koenigreich Boehmen am Anfang des XX. Jahrhunderts. Prague,* J.G. Calve'sche k.u.k. Hof- und Universitaets Buchhandlung, 1908.

Denar. (*Money*) Translated from the Czech, *Peníze* by D. A. Ogris. Ljubljana, Zvezna Tiskarna i Knjigarna, 1923.

Devalvace československé koruny. Devaluation of the Czechoslovak Crown. Prague, Československá Národní Banka, 1934. Also in English as *Devaluation of the Czechoslovak Crown;* in German, as *Die Devalvation der Tschechoslovakischen Krone,* and in French, as *La Devaluation de la couronne tchéchoslovaque.* Prague, Czechoslovak National Bank, 1934.

Economia Dirijata. Bucuresti: Biblioteca Monetara, Economica si Financiera, 1938. Rumanian translation of the Czech: *O řízeneém hospodářství*; see "Selected Bibliography," above.

"Hans Kelsens Lehre von der Gerechtigkeit," *Archives for Philosophy of Law and Social Philosophy,* 1961, XLVII: 3, 301-332. Prepared for publication by Ladislav A Fuerst.

Az Iranytott Gazasag. Budapest, Az Athenaeum Reszvenytarsulat, 1935. Hungarian translation of *O řízeném hospodářství*; see "Selected Bibliography," above.

"Karel Engliš: Kantův apriorism a myšlenkový řád" ("Karel Engliš: Apriorism in Kant and the Thought Order"). *Filosofický časopis.* Prague, 1967, 4, 531-543. An excerpt from the second volume of K. Engliš' as yet unpublished *Velká logika.* Prepared and provided with comments by Ladislav A. Fuerst.

Krize a ceny. (*Economic Crisis and Prices*). Prague, Fr. Borový, 1931.

Die Lehre von der Denkordnung. Wien: Rohrer-Verlag, 1961. A shorter essay based on Engliš' *Velká logika*, (*Major Logic*), which still remains largely in manuscript form.

Malá finanční věda. (*Introduction to the Science of Finance*). Prague, Fr. Borový, 1932. Also in Spanish as *Introduction a la Ciencia Financiera.* Translated by Dr. Milic Kybal. Barcelona, Editorial Labor, Section X Economia, 1937.

Malá logika. Věda o myšlenkovém řádu. (*Minor Logic. Science of Thought-Order*). Prague, Melantrich. 1947. Published in revised form in German as *Das Problem der Logik.* Wien: Rohrer-Verlag, 1961.

'Nemecký socialismus' jako program sudetoněmecké strany. Prague, Fr. Borový, 1938. Also in English as *'German Socialism' as Programme of the Helein Party; in French as 'Le socialism allemand' comme programme du parti henleinein;* and in German as *'Der deutsche Sozialismus' als Program der Sudetendeutschen Partei;* Prague, Orbis, 1938.

"Die Norm ist kein Urteil" ("A Norm is not a Judgement"). *Archives for Philosophy of Law and Social Philosophy.* 1964, L:3. 305-316. Prepared for publication by Ladislav A. Fuerst.

"O hodnotě a hodnocení" ("On Value and Valuation"), *Filosofický časopis.* Prague, 1967, 1, 117-131. Prepared for publication by Ladislav A. Fuerst.

O nouzi nadbytku. (*On Poverty in the Midst of Plenty.*) Prague, Fr. Borový, 1935.

Otázky a názory. (*Issues and Opinions*). Prague, Fr. Borový, 1926.

Příspěvky ke statistice národního školství. (*On the Statistics of Public Education*). Monograph. Prague, Zemský statistický úřad, 1906; VII/2. Also in German as *Beitraege zur Statistik des Volksschulwesens.* Prague, J.G. Calve'sche k.u.k. Hof- und Universitaets Buchhandeung, 1906.

Teleologische Theorie der Staatswirtschaft. Bruen, Rohrer-Verlag, 1933. Following the Czech *Teleologie* and its German translation (*Begruendung*), both published in 1930, this 1933 German version concentrates on teleological methodology as applied in the national economy. Its basic teachings can be found in the 1932 Czech *Theorie* and in their final formulation in the 1938 *Soustava.* (For full titles, see above "Selected Bibliography.")

"Theorie der Statistik der Verbrauchswirtschaft," *Statistische Monatsschrift.* Wien, 1916, 429-481. Also in Czech as a monograph: *Theorie statistiky spotřebního hospodářství.* (*Statistical Theory of Consumer Economy*). Brno, Ústřední spolek jednot učitelských na Morave, 1917.

Tři roky finanční politiky, 1926-1928. (*Three Years of Financial Policy*). Prague, Fr. Borový, 1930.

Věda v politice či politika ve vědě. (*Science in Politics or Politics in Science*). Prague, J. Otto, 1927.

Z výsledku sčítání závodů živnostenskych z 3.6. 1902 v království českém. (Results of the Census of Small-Trade Establishments in the Kingdon of Bohemia of June 3, 1902). Monograph. Prague, Zemský statistický úřad, 1907. Also in German: *Aus den Ergebnissen der Gewerblichen Betriebszaehlungen vom 3 Juni 1902 im Koenigreich Boehmen.* Prague, J.G. Calve'sche k.u.k. Hof- und Universitaetes Buchhandling, 1907.

Some reviews and comments on Englis' thought:

Chutil, Václav: "Bruenner Volkswirtschafts-theoretische Schule," *Universitas Brunensis 1919-1969.* Brno: Universitas Purkyniana Brunensis, 1969; pp. 373-377. Discusses theoretical developments in economic thought as they evolved at this University (known during 1919-1939 as Masaryk University). Chytil particularly points to Engliš' encyclopedic knowledge not only of economics, but also of the political and social sciences and his skillful applications of his theories to economic problems.

Fux, B.: "La science des Finances en Tchécolslovaquie," *Revue de Science et de Legislation financieres,* 1931, Octobre-Novembre-Decembre, 5-15. Fux praises the clarity and originality of Engliš' study of public finance, recommending its translation into French.

Kallab, Jaroslav: "Die Recht- und Wirtschaftsphilosophie an der Masaryk Universitaet," *Prager Rundschau,* 1930, 246-247. Kallab, Professor of law at Masaryk University praises particularly the clarity of Engliš' thought, its logical consistency and Engliš' innovative contribution to our knowledge of the process of human cognition in the field of social sciences.

Ritschl, H.: "Karel Engliš' Finanzwissenschaft." *Finanz Archiv,* 1933. Bd. 1/1, 176-77. The reviewer considers the teleological methodology developed by K. Engliš and applied in public finance as an unusually clearly defined and powerful tool of analysis.

Ulrich, H.: *Nationaloekonomie und Betriebswirtschaftslehre.* Bern, 1944. Professor Ulrich refers on p. 51 to Karel Engliš' writing on the national economy as an outstanding foundation of economic theory.

Vencovský, František: "Karel Engliš" in the series "Profily známých ekonomů ("Profiles of Known Economists"). (Prague, 1970?) pp. 330-384. Vencovský reviews the main premises of Engliš' teaching, their implications and significance for the present situation in Czechoslovakia.

Eva B. Polach, Librarian
Library of Congress, Washington, D.C.

July 1986

EAST EUROPEAN MONOGRAPHS

The *East European Monographs* comprise scholarly books on the history and civilization of Eastern Europe. They are published under the editorship of Stephen Fischer-Galati, in the belief that these studies contribute substantially to the knowledge of the area and serve to stimulate scholarship and research.

1. *Political Ideas and the Enlightenment in the Romanian Principalities,* 1750–1831. By Vlad Georgescu. 1971.
2. *America, Italy and the Birth of Yugoslavia, 1917–1919.* By Dragan R. Zivjinovic. 1972.
3. *Jewish Nobles and Geniuses in Modern Hungary.* By William O. McCagg, Jr. 1972.
4. *Mixail Soloxov in Yugoslavia: Reception and Literary Impact.* By Robert F. Price. 1973.
5. *The Historical and Nationalist Thought of Nicolae Iorga.* By William O. Oldson. 1973.
6. *Guide to Polish Libraries and Archives.* By Richard C. Lewanski. 1974.
7. *Vienna Broadcasts to Slovakia, 1938–1939: A Case Study in Subversion.* By Henry Delfiner. 1974.
8. *The 1917 Revolution in Latvia.* By Andrew Ezergailis. 1974.
9. *The Ukraine in the United Nations Organization: A Study in Soviet Foreign Policy. 1944–1950.* By Konstantin Sawczuk. 1975.
10. *The Bosnian Church: A New Interpretation.* By John V. A. Fine, Jr., 1975.
11. *Intellectual and Social Developments in the Habsburg Empire from Maria Theresa to World War I.* Edited by Stanley B. Winters and Joseph Held. 1975.
12. *Ljudevit Gaj and the Illyrian Movement.* By Elinor Murray Despalatovic. 1975.
13. *Tolerance and Movements of Religious Dissent in Eastern Europe,* Edited by Bela K. Kiraly. 1975.
14. *The Parish Republic: Hlinka's Slovak People's Party, 1939–1945.* By Yeshayahu Jelinek. 1976.
15. *The Russian Annexation of Bessarabia, 1774–1828.* By George F. Jewsbury. 1976.
16. *Modern Hungarian Historiography.* By Steven Bela Vardy. 1976.
17. *Values and Community in Multi-National Yugoslavia.* By Gary K. Bertsch. 1976.
18. *The Greek Socialist Movement and the First World War: the Road to Unity.* By George B. Leon. 1976.
19. *The Radical Left in the Hungarian Revolution of 1848.* By Laszlo Deme. 1976.
20. *Hungary between Wilson and Lenin: The Hungarian Revolution of 1918–1919 and the Big Three.* By Peter Pastor. 1976.

21. *The Crises of France's East-Central European Diplomacy, 1933–1938.* By Anthony J. Komjathy. 1976.
22. *Polish Politics and National Reform, 1775–1788.* By Daniel Stone. 1976.
23. *The Habsburg Empire in World War I.* Edited by Robert A. Kann, Bela K. Kiraly, and Paula S. Fichtner. 1977.
24. *The Slovenes and Yugoslavism, 1890–1914.* By Carole Rogel. 1977.
25. *German-Hungarian Relations and the Swabian Problem.* By Thomas Spira. 1977.
26. *The Metamorphosis of a Social Class in Hungary During the Reign of Young Franz Joseph.* By Peter I. Hidas. 1977.
27. *Tax Reform in Eighteenth Century Lombardy.* By Daniel M. Klang. 1977.
28. *Tradition versus Revolution: Russia and the Balkans in 1917.* By Robert H. Johnston. 1977.
29. *Winter into Spring: The Czechoslovak Press and the Reform Movement 1963–1968.* By Frank L. Kaplan. 1977.
30. *The Catholic Church and the Soviet Government, 1939–1949.* By Dennis J. Dunn. 1977.
31. *The Hungarian Labor Service System, 1939–1945.* By Randolph L. Braham. 1977.
32. *Consciousness and History: Nationalist Critics of Greek Society 1897–1914.* By Gerasimos Augustinos. 1977.
33. *Emigration in Polish Social and Political Thought, 1870–1914.* By Benjamin P. Murdzek. 1977.
34. *Serbian Poetry and Milutin Bojic.* By Mihailo Dordevic. 1977.
35. *The Baranya Dispute: Diplomacy in the Vortex of Ideologies, 1918–1921.* By Leslie C. Tihany. 1978.
36. *The United States in Prague, 1945–1948.* By Walter Ullmann. 1978.
37. *Rush to the Alps: The Evolution of Vacationing in Switzerland.* By Paul P. Bernard. 1978.
38. *Transportation in Eastern Europe: Empirical Findings.* By Bogdan Mieczkowski. 1978.
39. *The Polish Underground State: A Guide to the Underground, 1939–1945.* By Stefan Korbonski. 1978.
40. *The Hungarian Revolution of 1956 in Retrospect.* Edited by Bela K. Kiraly and Paul Jonas. 1978.
41. *Boleslaw Limanowski (1935–1935): A Study in Socialism and Nationalism.* By Kazimiera Janina Cottam. 1978.
42. *The Lingering Shadow of Nazism: The Austrian Independent Party Movement Since 1945.* By Max E. Riedlsperger. 1978.
43. *The Catholic Church, Dissent and Nationality in Soviet Lithuania.* By V. Stanley Vardys. 1978.
44. *The Development of Parliamentary Government in Serbia.* By Alex N. Dragnich. 1978.
45. *Divide and Conquer: German Efforts to Conclude a Separate Peace, 1914–1918.* By L. L. Farrar, Jr. 1978.
46. *The Prague Slav Congress of 1848.* By Lawrence D. Orton. 1978.
47. *The Nobility and the Making of the Hussite Revolution.* By John M. Klassen. 1978.
48. *The Cultural Limits of Revolutionary Politics: Change and Continuity in Socialist Czechoslovakia.* By David W. Paul. 1979.
49. *On the Border of War and Peace: Polish Intelligence and Diplomacy in 1937–1939 and the Origins of the Ultra Secret.* By Richard A. Woytak. 1979.
50. *Bear and Foxes: The International Relations of the East European States 1965–1969.* By Ronald Haly Linden. 1979.

51. *Czechoslovakia: The Heritage of Ages Past.* Edited by Ivan Volgyes and Hans Brisch. 1979.
52. *Prime Minister Gyula Andrassy's Influence on Habsburg Foreign Policy.* By Janos Decsy. 1979.
53. *Citizens for the Fatherland: Education, Educators, and Pedagogical Ideals in Eighteenth Century Russia.* By J. L. Black. 1979.
54. *A History of the "Proletariat": The Emergence of Marxism in the Kingdom of Poland, 1870–1887.* By Norman M. Naimark. 1979.
55. *The Slovak Autonomy Movement, 1935–1939: A Study in Unrelenting Nationalism.* By Dorothea H. El Mallakh. 1979.
56. *Diplomat in Exile: Francis Pulszky's Political Activities in England, 1849–1860.* By Thomas Kabdebo. 1979.
57. *The German Struggle Against the Yugoslav Guerrillas in World War II: German Counter-Insurgency in Yugoslavia, 1941–1943.* By Paul N. Hehn. 1979.
58. *The Emergence of the Romanian National State.* By Gerald J. Bobango. 1979.
59. *Stewards of the Land: The American Farm School and Modern Greece.* By Brenda L. Marder. 1979.
60. *Roman Dmowski: Party, Tactics, Ideology, 1895–1907.* By Alvin M. Fountain, II. 1980.
61. *International and Domestic Politics in Greece During the Crimean War.* By Jon V. Kofas. 1980.
62. *Fires on the Mountain: The Macedonian Revolutionary Movement and the Kidnapping of Ellen Stone.* By Laura Beth Sherman. 1980.
63. *The Modernization of Agriculture: Rural Transformation in Hungary, 1848–1975.* Edited by Joseph Held. 1980.
64. *Britain and the War for Yugoslavia, 1940–1943.* By Mark C. Wheeler. 1980.
65. *The Turn to the Right: The Ideological Origins and Development of Ukrainian Nationalism, 1919–1929.* By Alexander J. Motyl. 1980.
66. *The Maple Leaf and the White Eagle: Canadian-Polish Relations, 1918–1978.* By Aloysius Balawyder. 1980.
67. *Antecedents of Revolution: Alexander I and the Polish Congress Kingdom, 1815–1825.* By Frank W. Thackeray. 1980.
68. *Blood Libel at Tiszaeszlar.* By Andrew Handler. 1980.
69. *Democratic Centralism in Romania: A Study of Local Communist Politics.* By Daniel N. Nelson. 1980.
70. *The Challenge of Communist Education: A Look at the German Democratic Republic.* By Margrete Siebert Klein. 1980.
71. *The Fortifications and Defense of Constantinople.* By Byron C. P. Tsangadas. 1980.
72. *Balkan Cultural Studies.* By Stavro Skendi. 1980.
73. *Studies in Ethnicity: The East European Experience in America.* Edited by Charles A. Ward, Philip Shashko, and Donald E. Pienkos. 1980.
74. *The Logic of "Normalization:" The Soviet Intervention in Czechoslovakia and the Czechoslovak Response.* By Fred Eidlin. 1980.
75. *Red Cross. Black Eagle: A Biography of Albania's American Schol.* By Joan Fultz Kontos. 1981.
76. *Nationalism in Contemporary Europe.* By Franjo Tudjman. 1981.
77. *Great Power Rivalry at the Turkish Straits: The Montreux Conference and Convention of 1936.* By Anthony R. DeLuca. 1981.
78. *Islam Under the Double Eagle: The Muslims of Bosnia and Hercegovina, 1878–1914.* By Robert J. Donia. 1981.

79. *Five Eleventh Century Hungarian Kings: Their Policies and Their Relations with Rome.* By Z. J. Kosztolnyik. 1981.
80. *Prelude to Appeasement: East European Central Diplomacy in the Early 1930's.* By Lisanne Radice. 1981.
81. *The Soviet Regime in Czechoslovakia.* By Zdenek Krystufek. 1981.
82. *School Strikes in Prussian Poland, 1901–1907: The Struggle Over Bilingual Education.* By John J. Kulczychi. 1981.
83. *Romantic Nationalism and Liberalism: Joachim Lelewel and the Polish National Idea.* By Joan S. Skurnowicz. 1981.
84. *The "Thaw" In Bulgarian Literature.* By Atanas Slavov. 1981.
85. *The Political Thought of Thomas G. Masaryk.* By Roman Szporluk. 1981.
86. *Prussian Poland in the German Empire, 1871–1900.* By Richard Blanke. 1981.
87. *The Mazepists: Ukrainian Separatism in the Early Eighteenth Century.* By Orest Subtelny. 1981.
88. *The Battle for the Marchlands: The Russo-Polish Campaign of 1920.* By Adam Zamoyski. 1981.
89. *Milovan Djilas: A Revolutionary as a Writer.* By Dennis Reinhartz. 1981.
90. *The Second Republic: The Disintegration of Post-Munich Czechoslovakia, October 1938-March 1939.* By Theodore Prochazka, Sr. 1981.
91. *Financial Relations of Greece and the Great Powers, 1832–1862.* By Jon V. Kofas. 1981.
92. *Religion and Politics: Bishop Valerian Trifa and His Times.* By Gerald J. Bobango. 1981.
93. *The Politics of Ethnicity in Eastern Europe.* Edited by George Klein and Milan J. Reban. 1981.
94. *Czech Writers and Politics.* By Alfred French. 1981.
95. *Nation and Ideology: Essays in Honor of Wayne S. Vucinich.* Edited by Ivo Banac, John G. Ackerman, and Roman Szporluk. 1981.
96. *For God and Peter the Great: The Works of Thomas Consett, 1723–1729.* Edited by James Cracraft. 1982.
97. *The Geopolitics of Leninism.* By Stanley W. Page. 1982
98. *Karel Havlicek (1821–1856): A National Liberation Leader of the Czech Renascence.* By Barbara K. Reinfeld. 1982.
99. *Were-Wolf and Vampire in Romania.* By Harry A. Senn. 1982.
100. *Ferdinand I of Austria: The Politics of Dynasticism in the Age of Reformation.* By Paula Sutter Fichtner. 1982.
101. *France in Greece During World War I: A Study in the Politics of Power.* By Alexander S. Mitrakos. 1982.
102. *Authoritarian Politics in a Transitional State: Istvan Bethlen and the Unified Party in Hungary, 1919–1926.* By William M. Batkay. 1982.
103. *Romania Between East and West: Historical Essays in Memory of Constantin C. Giurescu.* Edited by Stephen Fischer-Galati, Radu R. Florescu and George R. Ursul. 1982.
104. *War and Society in East Central Europe: From Hunyadi to Rakoczi—War and Society in Late Medieval and Early Modern Hungary.* Edited by János Bak and Béla K. Király. 1982.
105. *Total War and Peace Making: A Case Study on Trianon.* Edited by Béla K. Király, Peter Pastor, and Ivan Sanders. 1982
106. *Army, Aristocracy, and Monarchy: Essays on War, Society, and Government in Austria, 1618–1780.* Edited by Wayne S. Vucinich. 1982.
107. *The First Serbian Uprising, 1804–1813.* Edited by Wayne S. Vucinich. 1982.

108. *Propaganda and Nationalism in Wartime Russia: The Jewish Anti-Fascist Committee in the USSR, 1941–1948.* By Shimon Redich. 1982.
109. *One Step Back, Two Steps Forward: On the Language Policy of the Communist Party of Soviet Union in the National Republics.* By Michael Bruchis. 1982.
110. *Bessarabia and Bukovina: The Soviet-Romanian Territorial Dispute.* by Nicholas Dima. 1982
111. *Greek-Soviet Relations, 1917–1941.* By Andrew L. Zapantis. 1982.
112. *National Minorities in Romania: Change in Transylvania.* By Elemer Illyes. 1982.
113. *Dunarea Noastra: Romania, the Great Powers, and the Danube Question, 1914–1921.* by Richard C. Frucht. 1982.
114. *Continuity and Change in Austrian Socialism: The Eternal Quest for the Third Way.* By Melanie A. Sully. 1982
115. *Catherine II's Greek Prelate: Eugenios Voulgaris in Russia, 1771–1806.* By Stephen K. Batalden. 1982.
116. *The Union of Lublin: Polish Federalism in the Golden Age.* By Harry E. Dembkowski. 1982.
117. *Heritage and Continuity in Eastern Europe: The Transylvanian Legacy in the History of the Romanians.* By Cornelia Bodea and Virgil Candea. 1982.
118. *Contemporary Czech Cinematography: Jiri Menzel and the History of The "Closely Watched Trains".* By Josef Skvorecky. 1982.
119. *East Central Europe in World War I: From Foreign Domination to National Freedom.* By Wiktor Sukiennicki. 1982.
120. *City, Town, and Countryside in the Early Byzantine Era.* Edited by Robert L. Hohlfelder. 1982.
121. *The Byzantine State Finances in the Eighth and Ninth Centuries.* By Warren T. Treadgold. 1982.
122. *East Central European Society and War in Pre-Revolutionary Eighteenth Century.* Edited by Gunther E. Rothenberg, Bela K. Kiraly and Peter F. Sugar. 1982.
123. *Czechoslovak Policy and the Hungarian Minority, 1945–1948.* By Kalman Janics. 1982.
124. *At the Brink of War and Peace: The Tito-Stalin Split in a Historic Perspective.* Edited by Wayne S. Vucinich. 1982.
125. *The Road to Bellapais: The Turkish Cypriot Exodus to Northern Cyprus.* By Pierre Oberling. 1982.
126. *Essays on World War I: Origins and Prisoners of War.* Edited by Peter Pastor and Samuel R. Williamson, Jr. 1983.
127. *Panteleimon Kulish: A Sketch of His Life and Times.* By George S. N. Luckyj. 1983.
128. *Economic Development in the Habsburg Monarchy in the Nineteenth Century: Essays.* Edited by John Komlos. 1983.
129. *Warsaw Between the World Wars: Profile of the Capital City in a Developing Land, 1918–1939.* By Edward D. Wynot, Jr. 1983.
130. *The Lust for Power: Nationalism, Slovakia, and The Communists, 1918–1948.* By Yeshayahu Jelinek. 1983.
131. *The Tsar's Loyal Germans: The Riga German Community: Social Change and the Nationality Question, 1855–1905.* By Anders Henriksson. 1983.
132. *Society in Change: Studies in Honor of Bela K. Kiraly.* Edited by Steven Bela Vardy. 1983.
133. *Authoritariansim in Greece: The Metaxas Regime.* By Jon V. Kofas. 1983.
134. *New Hungarian Peasants: An East Central European Experience with Collectivization.* Edited by Marida Hollos and Bela C. Maday. 1983.

135. *War, Revolution, and Society in Romania: The Road to Independence*. Edited by Ilie Ceausescu. 1983.
136. *The Beginning of Cyrillic Printing, Cracow, 1491: From the Orthodox Past in Poland*. By Szczepan K. Zimmer. 1983.
137. *Effects of World War I. The Class War After the Great War: The Rise of Communist Parties in East Central Europe, 1918–1921*. Edited by Ivo Banac. 1983.
138. *Bulgaria 1878–1918. A History*. By Richard J. Crampton. 1983.
139. *T. G. Masaryk Revisited: A Cirtical Assessment*. By Hanus J. Hajek. 1983.
140. *The Cult of Power: Dictators in the Twentieth Century*. Edited by Joseph Held. 1983.
141. *Economy and Foreign Policy: The Struggle of the Great Powers for Economic Hegemony in the Danube Valley, 1919–1939*. By György Ránki. 1983.
142. *Germany, Russia, and the Balkans: Prelude to the Nazi-Soviet Non-Aggression Pact*. By Marilynn Giroux Hitchens. 1983.
143. Guestworkers in the German Reich: The Poles in Wilhelmian Germany. By Richard Charles Murphy. 1983.
144. *The Latvian Impact on the Bolshevik Revolution*. By Andrew Ezergailis. 1983.
145. *The Rise of Moscow's Power*. By Henryk Paszkiewicz. 1983.
146. *A Question of Empire: Leopold I and the War of the Spanish Succession, 1701–1705*. By Linda and Marsha Frey. 1983.
147. *Effects of World War I. The Uprooted: Hungarian Refugees and Their Impact on Hungarian Domestic Policies, 1918–1921*. By Istvan I. Mocsy. 1983.
148. *Nationalist Integration Through Socialist Planning: An Anthropological Study of a Romanian New Town*. By Steven L. Sampson. 1983.